Illustrated SERMONS for Special Occasions

J. B. FOWLER, JR.

BROADMAN PRESS
Nashville, Tennessee

© Copyright 1988 • Broadman Press
All rights reserved
4222-65
ISBN: 0-8054-2265-X
Dewey Decimal Classification: 252.6
Subject Headings: SERMONS—COLLECTED WORKS //
HOLIDAYS—COLLECTED WORKS
Library of Congress Catalog Card Number: 87-14297
Printed in the United States of America

All Scripture quotations are from the King James Version of the Bible.

Library of Congress Cataloging-in-Publication Data

Fowler, J. B., 1930-
  Illustrated sermons for special occasions.

  1. Occasional sermons—Outlines, syllabi, etc.
2. Homiletical illustrations. I. Title.
BV4223.F66   1988   252′.6   87-14297

Foreword

I am grateful to Dr. J. B. Fowler, Jr. for giving me the privilege of writing the "Foreword" of his latest book in his "illustrated" group of books. His previous books are *Living Illustrations* and *Illustrated Sermon Outlines*.

Prior to assuming the position as editor of the *Baptist New Mexican* he was a pastor for thirty years. He is familiar with the problem of pastors in finding fresh material for sermons on special occasions. This is especially acute in long pastorates. This volume is designed to be helpful in meeting that need.

For over thirty years Dr. Fowler has been an avid collector of good illustrations. As we remember best Jesus' teachings through parables, so do we remember the messages in sermons which are presented through modern *parables* or illustrations drawn from everyday life. This book is a gold mine of such.

This volume will prove beneficial to pastors and Sunday School teachers. Also it provides good devotional reading for all of us.

Actually the book is one of sermons for special days and occasions. Each sermon is filled with apt illustrations. They contain fresh illustrative material which will gladden every pastor's heart.

I predict for it a wide readership. We are in Dr. Fowler's debt for his sharing with us the fruits of his labors through the years.

HERSCHEL H. HOBBS

Pastor Emeritus,
First Baptist Church,
Oklahoma City, Oklahoma

This volume is lovingly dedicated
to my two sons, Bruce and David,
and to Bruce's wife, Joyce,
and to their son, Reid.

Author's Preface

The late Vance Havner wrote: "There's a lot of cheap preaching going around over the country. I heard of a preacher some years ago when haircuts were selling for 50 cents who had a barber in the crowd who said, 'I'll cut your hair for nothing. I'll take it out in preaching.'

"The preacher said, 'Well, I'll have you know that I don't preach any 50-cent sermons!' And the barber said, 'That's all right, I'll come several times.' "[1]

As I finish this volume of *Illustrated Sermons for Special Occasions*, I don't know what price Broadman Press will put on the book, but I hope these sermons don't fall under the category of "cheap preaching." Although the sermons are not as honed and polished as they might be, perhaps they will help a fellow preacher put together a sermon or two for some special occasion. My experience in preaching for nearly forty years is that the special days give me problems. Serving as a pastor of one church for ten years, it became a bit difficult to come up with ten fresh sermons on Christmas or Labor Day. So, maybe these messages will give a preacher somewhere a new idea or two for those special days that tax us.

I am indebted to Dr. H. H. Hobbs, Oklahoma City, for the gracious foreword he has written to this book. A past president of the Southern Baptist Convention, loved and respected by Baptists across the nation, to have Dr. Hobbs write the foreword has brought immeasurable joy to my heart. I have the utmost respect for him and express my gratitude to him.

Also, I owe an immense debt of gratitude to my secretary, Jana Boley, who carefully typed the manuscripts. Her kind attitude and

sweet spirit, coupled with her typing skill, have contributed greatly to making this volume possible.

As the reader will quickly discover, the sermons are heavy on
illustrations. Many illustrations have been included—at times, perhaps, too many—with the hope that they will stoke some
preacher's sermonic coals and set him on the path to preparing a
fresh sermon for some special occasion.

Note

1. From *Proclaim*, July-Sept. (p. 38). © Copyright 1976, The, Sunday School
Board of the Southern Baptist Convention. All rights reserved. Used by permission.

Contents

Divine Demands for a New Year

Scripture: Colossians 3:1-15

Introduction

Have you ever wondered why the picture of the dog listening to an old gramophone appears on RCA records? You have probably also wondered about the words beneath the logo, "His Master's Voice."

Francis Barraud, an English artist who lived at Kensington-on-Thames, had a dog named Nipper. A smooth-haired, fox terrier, Nipper was intelligent and much loved by Barraud.

When Edison astonished the world in 1877 with his invention of the phonograph, Barraud painted a picture of the dog intently listening to gramophone. Sending the painting to a new electronics company in the United States that was gearing up to produce records for Edison's new invention, Barraud suggested that they use the picture of the dog and carry the caption beneath it, "His Master's Voice."

But the company wasn't interested in Barraud's proposal and did nothing about it. Thirty years later, Barraud touched up the old painting of Nipper and sent it back to the company. They accepted Barraud's proposal and it has appeared on RCA records since that time. And Nipper made Barraud a wealthy man.

When Paul wrote to the Colossians, he told them they must listen to their Master's voice. Jesus was their Lord. They were His followers. As such He made some demands upon them to which they must be obedient.

As we approach the beginning of a new year, these divine demands about which Paul wrote to the Colossians are as binding upon us today as they were upon the Colossians. These are not suggestions from the Savior; they are divine demands.

As I look at the passage, three divine demands for a new year surface.

We Must Love What Is Good (vv. 1-4)

Raffaello Sanzio, known by lovers of art as Raphael, was one of history's greatest artists and painters. He was called the "Divine Raphael."

His *Sistine Madonna*, completed in 1515, hangs in the Dresden Gallery in Germany. But when the picture was first brought to Dresden, it was placed in the Throne Room of the castle. But the throne occupied the most conspicuous place in the room and the king wasn't satisfied to display the *Madonna* in a less favorable place. So, pushing the throne to one side, the king said, "Make room for the immortal Raphael." And Raphael's *Madonna* was placed in the most prestigious place in the Throne Room.

Love for Jesus Christ compels us to give Him first place in our lives. It motivates us to love what is good, as Jesus did.

The reason for it.—"Risen with Christ" (v. 1); "For ye are dead, and your life is hid with Christ in God" (v. 3).

The way to it.—"Set your affection on things above, not on things on the earth" (v. 2). "Set" is in the present tense: "Keep on thinking about" (A. T. Robertson); "For ye are dead" (v. 3) is aorist, looking back to a past, definite experience; "Is hid" (v. 3) is perfect passive: concealed in the past and still concealed.

The reward of it.—"When Christ, who is our life, shall appear, then shall ye also appear with him in glory" (v. 4). Our eternal life is "the motivating energy and directive agent of the new kind of life" the believer lives (Wuest).

In obeying these divine demands for a new year:

We Must Shun What Is Wrong (vv. 5-11)

"When Charles Spurgeon was once being shown through the library of Trinity College, Cambridge, he stopped to admire a bust of Byron. The librarian said to him, 'Stand here, sir, and look at it.'

"Spurgeon took the position indicated and, looking upon the bust, remarked, 'What an intellectual countenance! What a grand genius!'

" 'Come now,' said the librarian, 'and look at it from this side.'

"Spurgeon changed his position and, looking on the statue from that viewpoint, exclaimed, 'What a demon! There stands a man who could defy the Deity!' He asked the librarian if the sculptor had secured this effect designedly.

" 'Yes,' he replied, 'he wished to picture the two characters, the two persons—the great, the grand, the almost supergenius that he possessed; and yet the enormous mass of sin that was in his soul.' "[1]

There are two natures within the Christian: the divine nature and the sinful nature. And if the Christian is going to shun what is wrong one must daily live under the lordship of Jesus Christ.

We must shun sins that would defeat us.—"Mortify" (v. 5)—immediately, permanently—and the list includes the grossest sins of the flesh (v. 5). "Put off" (v. 8)—aorist imperative: immediately—"lay aside like old clothes" (A. T. Robertson). "Put off" (v. 9)—aorist: immediately, decisively: "having stripped clean off" (A. T. Robertson).

We are told how to do it.—"And have put on the new man, which is renewed" (v. 10). At a definite time in the past we took on a new life, as one would put on a garment. This new man is "[being] renewed" (v. 10.)—present tense: "It is a continual refreshment of the new man in Christ Jesus" (A. T. Robertson). "Put on" (v. 12)—aorist imperative: a command to be obeyed immediately, decisively.

These divine demands for a new day show us:

We Must Do What Is Right (vv. 12-15)

Author George Eliot said: "Ideas are poor things until they become incarnate." We must practice what we know is right.

Who of us has not been moved by Millet's paintings, *The Angelus, The Gleaners,* and *Man with the Hoe?*

Born near Cherbourg, France, in 1814, Millet was sent to Paris by the citizens of his hometown to study under the noted painter, Paul Delaroche. Just before Millet left home, his godly grandmother told him: "I had rather see you dead than unfaithful to God's commands." After he had become a famous painter, she warned him: "Remember, my son, you were a Christian before you became a painter." He was expected to do what was right because he was a Christian.

Paul lists several things that are right:
1. We must live compassionately (v. 12).
2. We must live forgivingly (v. 13).
3. We must live lovingly (v. 14).
4. We must live peaceably (v. 15).

Conclusion

On his last birthday, missionary David Livingstone wrote in his diary: "Lord Jesus, my king, my life, my all, I again dedicate my whole self to thee." That is the spirit each of us must have as we face Christ's divine demands for this new year that lies before us.

When Queen Elizabeth II became queen of England on February 8, 1952, she received a gracious letter from her grandmother, Queen Mary the widow of King George V.

The grandmother signed her letter to the new, young Queen Elizabeth with the words, "Your loving grandmother and devoted subject."

As followers of Jesus, we must have that kind of obedient attitude to Him. If we do, the new year will mean all God intends it to mean.

Note

1. Clarence Macartney, *Macartney's Illustrations* (New York, Nashville: Abingdon-Cokesbury Press, 1945), p. 221.

Watching Jesus on the Cross

Scripture: Matthew 27:36

Introduction

A popular monk of the Middle Ages was asked to preach a sermon on the love of God. He was scheduled to preach on a certain evening in a large cathedral and when the time came for the service to begin, the cathedral was overflowing with people anxious to hear their popular monk. As the last rays of evening light faded from the cathedral windows, the monk walked over to a large candelabrum near the altar and removed a lighted candle. Then, walking up to the large crucifix of Jesus in the altar, the monk held the candle so that the people could see the wounds in the hands, feet, side, and brow of Jesus. Then without saying a word, the monk placed the candle back in the candelabrum and left the cathedral. And the people in the community agreed that the monk's message on the love of God was one of the most moving and eloquent messages they had ever heard.

The central theme of the New Testament is the crucifixion and resurrection of Jesus Christ. It is mentioned in every book of the New Testament except Philemon, 2 John, and 3 John. And on this Good Friday we come back to the central teaching of the New Testament as we watch Jesus on the cross.

Hanging in the National Gallery of Art in Washington D.C., is Raphael's painting *The Alba Madonna*. Painted by the Italian master in 1510, it is one of the most beautiful examples of Italian Renaissance painting still in existence. The Christ child, with a small cross in his hand, is sitting on Mary's lap. She has her arm around the young child John. All eyes in the painting are on the cross. The cross is central.

In the New Testament the cross is central. Matthew takes 141 verses to describe the crucifixion. The short Gospel of Mark contains 116 verses about the crucifixion. Luke describes the arrest and crucifixion in two long chapters. And one half of John's Gospel deals with the events at the close of Christ's earthly life.

On this Good Friday, as we look toward Easter, and the glorious resurrection of our Savior, our thoughts are on the cross. Nearly two thousand years ago, on another Good Friday, Jesus was nailed to the cross that we might be saved. And now today, in this simple worship service, we shall watch Jesus on the cross.

As we watch Jesus on the cross:

We See Jesus Praying

"Then said Jesus, Father, forgive them; for they know not what they do. And they parted his raiment, and cast lots" (Luke 23:34).

Last words are important. Mussolini, the Italian dictator, sputtered as he was being dragged to his execution: "But . . . but . . . Mr. Colonel!" Ethan Allen, American Revolutionary hero, when told the angels were waiting for him, shouted: "Waiting are they? Waiting are they? Well . . . let them wait!" Toward the end, Beethoven sighed: "Too bad! Too late!" Marie Antoinette appologized to her executioner and Charles II of England spoke of his mistress, Nell Gwyn. Confederate General Robert E. Lee sighed, "Strike the tents!" Saint Francis of Assisi said, "Welcome, sister death!" And Thomas Jefferson, writer of the Declaration of Independence, said: "Now let they servant depart in peace." And among the seven last words spoken by Jesus was this prayer, "Father, forgive them; for they know not what they do" (Luke 23:34).

Notice where He prayed.—Soldiers have prayed on fields of battle; sailors have prayed as their ships sank into the deep; pilots have prayed as their planes screamed toward the earth; children have prayed by the sides of their beds; mothers have prayed in the kitchen; fathers have prayed as they worked in the field; and sinners have prayed at church, but Jesus prayed on the cross. The key to where Jesus prayed is the first word of verse 34: "Then said Jesus, Father, forgive them." When sin had done its worst, then Jesus prayed. When hate had nailed Him to the tree, then Jesus prayed. When He had been spat upon, unjustly judged, cruelly crowned, publicly flogged, and openly crucified, then Jesus prayed!

Notice for whom He prayed.—A. T. Robertson (*Word Pictures in the New Testament*) has an interesting note: "Jesus evidently is praying for the Roman soldiers, who were only obeying, but not for the Sanhedrin." Unlike the Sanhedrin, the Roman soldiers were surely those who "know not what they do." But I interpret this prayer personally: Jesus prayed for all sinners in all ages whose sins had nailed Him to the cross.

As we watch Jesus on the cross:

We See Jesus Suffering

Read how James M. Stalker described the crucifixion: "The cross was most probably of the form in which it is usually represented— an upright post crossed by a bar near the top. . . . The arms were probably bound to the cross-beam, as without this the hands would have been torn through by the weight. And for a similar reason there was a piece of wood projecting from the middle of the upright beam, on which the body sat. The feet were either nailed separately or crossed the one over the other, with a nail through both. . . . The head hung free, so that the dying man could both see and speak to those about the cross.

"In modern executions the greatest pains are taken to make death as nearly as possible instantaneous. . . . But the most revolting feature of death by crucifixion was that the torture was deliberately prolonged. The victim usually lingered a whole day, sometimes two or three days, still retaining consciousness; while the burning of the wounds in the hands and feet, the uneasiness of the unnatural position, the oppression of overcharged veins and, above all, the intolerable thirst were constantly increasing."[1]

But the greatest sufferings of Jesus were not physical, they were spiritual. He had taken upon Himself our guilt.

He suffered as a sinner.—"At about the ninth hour Jesus cried with a loud voice, saying, Eli, Eli lama sabachthani? that is to say, My God, my God, why hast thou forsaken me?" (Matt. 27:46). "The reproaches of them that reproached thee fell on me" (Rom. 15:3).

He suffered in place of sinners.—"For Christ also hath once suffered for sins, the just for the unjust, that he might bring us to God, being put to death in the flesh, but quickened by the Spirit" (1 Pet. 3:18). In Stroudsburg, Pennsylvania, there is a grave for a

Yankee soldier who fell during the Civil War. The soldier's name, birth, and death are cut on the stone along with these words: "Abraham Lincoln's substitute." During that hideous war in which 400 men died every day for four long years, Lincoln realized that those soldiers were dying for him. To honor all of them, he honored one fallen comrade. On that soldier's headstone Lincoln had his name carved as a tribute to the men who had died for him.

At the cross:

We See Jesus Saving

Jesus summed up His ministry when He said to Zacchaeus: "For the Son of man is come to seek and to save that which was lost" (Luke 19:10). At the cross He did the very thing for which He had come: He saved the soul of a sinner. The penitent thief said to Jesus: "Lord, remember me when thou comest into thy kingdom." And Jesus replied: "Verily I say unto thee, today shalt thou be with me in paradise" (Luke 23:42-43).

Jesus is always willing to save.—The thief was saved at death's door. Although Jesus will save one at death's door, it is wise not to put it off that long, for death may come unannounced. "Now is the accepted time; behold, now is the day of salvation" (2 Cor. 6:2).

Jesus is ready to save when we meet the conditions.—Repentance and faith are the conditions (Mark 1:14-15). Repentance and faith always go together; they cannot be separated. Where there is one, there is always the other. They are mutually inclusive (John 1:12; John 3:16; Rom. 10:9-10; Acts 16:31; Rom. 5:1). The thief's attitude as he approached Jesus demonstrated his sincere repentance from his sin and his sincere faith in the Savior.

At the cross, finally:

We See Jesus Dying

"Now there was set a vessel full of vinegar: and they filled a sponge with vinegar, and put it upon hyssop, and put it to his mouth. When Jesus therefore had received the vinegar, he said, It is finished: and he bowed his head, and gave up the ghost (John 19:29-30). "And when Jesus had cried with a loud voice, he said,

Father, into thy hands I commend my spirit: and having said thus, he gave up the ghost" (Luke 23:46).

He died voluntarily.—Jesus had said: "I lay down my life for the sheep. . . . Therefore doth my father love me, because I lay down my life, that I might take it again. No man taketh it from me, but I lay it down of myself. I have power to lay it down, and I have power to take it again" (John 10:15, 17-18). Luke 23:46 says that Jesus "gave up the ghost." About this, the *Expositor's Greek Testament* says: "Various shades of meaning have been put on the words, among which is that Jesus died by a free act of will, handing over his soul to God as a deposit to be kept."

He died confidently.—"Father, into thy hands I commend my spirit" (Luke 23:46). Jesus knew that upon death He would "depart out of this world unto the Father" (John 13:1). And He confidently committed His spirit unto His heavenly Father. He gives us an example of how a believer should die.

Conclusion

In George Bernard Shaw's play *Joan of Arc*, they take the maid of Orleans out to be burned at the stake. Knowing how her death will affect people in time to come, Joan says: "If I go through the fire, I shall go through it to their hearts forever and ever."

Jesus knew that about His cross. Although He dreaded the cross and pulled back from it as any human would do, Christ gladly and voluntarily suffered and died on the cross because He knew it was the one key that would unlock the hearts of sinners to receive Him.

David A. MacLennan, in *Resources for Sermon Preparation*, tells about a policeman—a "bobbie"—who found a small boy one day crying as though his heart had broken. When the bobbie asked the lad what was the problem and if he could help, the little boy replied that he was lost.

"Well," the bobbie said, "you must not cry. Just tell me where you live and I will help you find your way home."

And the little boy replied through sobs: "Just take me up the hill to that place where the white cross stands. If I can see the cross then I will be able to find my way home."

Mankind is lost without Jesus—away from home—and cannot

find the way back. But if we can only lead lost people to the cross, it will direct them home to God.

Note

1. James M. Stalker, *The Trial and Death of Jesus Christ* (Grand Rapids: Zondervan Publishing Co., 1984), pp. 99-100.

Easter's Encouragement

Scripture: Matthew 28:5-6

Introduction

Newspaper cartoonist H. T. Webster relates that he amused himself one day by sending congratulatory telegrams to twenty of his friends. Although none of them had done anything outstanding for which to be congratulated, Webster sent each the one-word message, "Congratulations." And each, in turn, wrote Webster a thank-you note without questioning why the message had been sent.

Everyone needs encouragement. But there is no encouragement that measures up to the encouragement Easter brings. Based on fact and not fantasy, Easter's encouragement is fresh and new every morning as the presence of the living Lord overshadows the believer.

The most encouraging news that has ever been heard on earth was the announcement of the angel to Mary Magdelene, Mary, and Salome: "Ye seek Jesus, which was crucified. He is not here: for he is risen. . . . Come, see the place where the Lord lay" (Matt. 28:5-6).

On this Easter morning, let me show you four ways in which Easter encourages us. First, it shows us:

Our Faith Hasn't Been Misplaced

The disciples had been with Jesus about three years. They had seen His miracles, heard His messages, and accepted Him as the Son of God. But when He was nailed to the cross, their faith crumbled about them for they thought it was the end of everything. When He was raised from the dead on Easter morning, however, they marched out from behind their closed doors to capture the world for their Lord. His resurrection validated their

17

belief in Him: "And declared to be the Son of God with power, according to the spirit of holiness, by the resurrection from the dead" (Rom. 1:4). When they saw their Lord alive, they knew that their faith hadn't been misplaced.

The late A. J. Cronin, a physician and writer, tells in his short story, "A Candle in Vienna," about walking the streets of Vienna shortly after the close of World War II. It was a bitterly cold day and as he saw the gutted, bombed-out city, his anger grew at what war had done. Slipping into a small quiet Catholic church at twilight, he observed that the building was dark except for a lone candle burning on the altar. Hearing a noise, he looked around to see an old, poor, shabbily dressed man walking down the aisle carrying a little girl in his arms. The two knelt together at the altar to pray. Then, after a few minutes, the old man picked up the crippled little girl and carried her back out to the street. Placing her in a homemade cart, the old man spread a potato sack across her frail body to shelter her from the biting wind. When Cronin asked the old man why they had come to the church, and if they came often, the old man replied that they came every day to pray and then he explained that the little girl's parents had been killed in the bombing of Vienna. "We come," the old man said, "to show God we are not angry with him." Their daily visits to the church kept their faith alive.

Secondly, Easter shows us that:

Our Lord Hasn't Forsaken Us

John said that the disciples, feeling they were forsaken and fearing lest they share the Lord's fate, hid behind closed doors in the upper room in Jerusalem: "Then the same day at evening, being the first day of the week, when the doors were shut where the disciples were assembled for fear of the Jews" (John 20:19). But with the resurrection of Jesus on Easter morning, they knew they had not been forsaken by their beloved Master: "Be content with such things as ye have: for he hath said, I will never leave thee, nor forsake thee" (Heb. 13:5). Because of His resurrection, Jesus now lives in each believer's life through His Holy Spirit (Acts 1:4; John 14:23-26; 16:7).

Abraham Lincoln, the sixteenth president of the United States, was shot on Good Friday, April 14, 1865, by John Wilkes Booth. Lincoln was sitting with his party in the presidential box at Ford's Theater when Booth quietly opened the door to the box and walked up behind the President. Just as Mary Lincoln took the President's hand in hers, Booth fired his small pistol at Lincoln's head. They carried the President across the street to a home owned by William Peterson, where Lincoln died the next morning at 7:22 AM. Secretary of War, Edwin Stanton, who had been kneeling by the President's bed, pulled down the shades on the windows and closed the half-opened eyes of Lincoln. Then Stanton said, "Now he belongs to the ages."

Because of His resurrection, Jesus, the living, conquering Lord, belongs to the ages and shall live in the lives of dedicated believers until time is no more. He hasn't forsaken us.

Thirdly, Easter encourages us by showing us that:

Our Life Doesn't End with the Grave

Jesus had told His disciples during His earthly ministry: "The Son of man shall be betrayed into the hands of men: And they shall kill him, and the third day he shall be raised again. And they were exceeding sorry" (Matt. 17:22-23). But the disciples didn't understand: "And they kept that saying with themselves, questioning one with another what the rising from the dead should mean" (Mark 9:10). John adds: "For as yet they knew not the scripture, that he must rise from the dead" (John 20:9). But His resurrection on Easter morning proved to all that life does not end with the grave: "I am he that liveth, and was dead; and, behold, I am alive for evermore, Amen; and have the keys of hell and of death" (Rev. 1:18).

William Makepeace Thackeray, the nineteenth-century British novelist, wrote a novel titled *The Newcomes*. The novel was published in 1855.

"Colonel Newcome, a kind-hearted soldier and an old-fashioned gentleman, lost his fortune and died in an almshouse.

"But before the colonel died, Thackeray showed him in bed with his hands outside the bedcovers. The fingers were gently moving, beating time to the nearby chapel bell ringing the evening hours.

"As the bell struck its last sound, Newcome's face lighted up and a smile played across his lips. Lifting his head just a little from the snowy pillow, he feebly said, *"Adsum,"* and fell back dead.

"It is a Latin word which means 'present.' It was the word Newcome and his school friends had used when they were children, and the roll was being called at school.

"Although the colonel was old and feeble, he again had the heart of a child; as he hears the Master calling the heavenly roll, he answered *'Adsum'* as his name was called."[1]

Finally, Easter encourages us by showing us that:

Our Tomorrows Will Be Better Than Today

The darkness of Good Friday wasn't the end of the story, for the sorrow of the disciples was swallowed up by the joy of Easter morning. Christians know that in Christ our tomorrows will always be better than our todays: "Let not your heart be troubled: ye believe in God, believe also in me. In my Father's house are many mansions: if it were not so, I would have told you. I go to prepare a place for you. And if I go and prepare a place for you, I will come again, and receive you unto myself; that where I am, there ye may be also" (John 14:1-3).

The late R. L. Middleton told about a young medical student who set up his practice in the mountains of Kentucky where the needs were great. He was in constant demand and faithfully rode the mountain trails wherever need called. He was a friend to all—birthing babies, caring for little children, and standing by the bedside when the elderly drew their last breath. When a terrible flu epidemic hit the mountain community, the doctor didn't slacken his pace. He cared for his patients day and night until he became ill. When he saw that he couldn't live, his last act was to thumb through his ledger and write in his own hand, "Paid in Full," over the bills of the people who owed him money.

After he died, the people of the community gathered for his memorial service. They buried him in a barren, little cemetery on the hillside and brought stones with their own hands to lay over his resting place. Someone then went into town, took down the sign that pointed up the stairs to the doctor's office, and on top of the stones placed the sign: "Dr. Mansfield. Office Upstairs."

Death doesn't end our work for Jesus. We shall carry on—"office upstairs"—and all our tomorrows will grow better and better in His home above.

Conclusion

Charlotte, Emily, and Anne Bronte were the daughters of an Irish clergyman. Charlotte (1816-1855), is probably best remembered for her book, *Jane Eyre*. When artist George Richmond was painting Charlotte's portrait, which many critics say is his finest work, he was unable to catch Charlotte's features as he wished, because her face was lined with despair. Richmond was about to give up when he remembered that one of Charlotte's heroes was Arthur Wellesley, the Duke of Wellington, who had defeated Napoleon at Waterloo on June 18, 1815.

Richmond had also been working the very morning on which he was painting Bronte's portrait on a portrait of the Duke, and when Richmond mentioned Wellington, Bronte's face lighted up with joy and delight. Working quickly, Richmond caught her joyous expression on canvas. This, authorities say, explains Richmond's masterpiece.

Jesus is the joy and inspiration of every believer. And the very mention of His name, and His glorious resurrection from the dead on the first Easter morning, puts a song in our hearts and floods our faces with joy.

Note
1. J. B. Fowler Jr., *Living Illustrations* (Nashville: Broadman Press, 1985), pp. 70-71.

A Magnificent Mother

Scripture: 1 Samuel 2:18-19

Introduction

At Ponca City, Oklahoma, there is a magnificent memorial named *The Pioneer Woman.* As a small boy, that statue of the pioneer woman made an indelible impression upon me.

There she stands in all her bronzed glory. In one hand she holds a Bible, and with the other she grasps the hand of her little son. Her eyes gaze off into the distance as though she is trying to see what lies ahead. She is a memorial to the pioneer women who helped open the West.

The memorial was sculpted by Bryant Baker, a European sculptor. E. W. Marlin, a former governor of Oklahoma, commissioned Baker to sculpt the magnificent masterpiece to motherhood.

But in this Mother's Day message, we are considering another magnificent mother. Her name was Hannah, the mother of the prophet Samuel. Her influence upon her son, and upon all history, can never be measured.

The biography of Hannah shows us several characteristics a truly magnificent mother possesses.

Magnificent in Prayer

The late Lee R. Scarborough was one of the presidents of Southwestern Baptist Theological Seminary in Fort Worth, Texas.

In his biography about Scarborough, H. E. Dana wrote that Scarborough's mother wanted him to be a minister. When Scarborough was only three years old, his mother became seriously ill. Too weak to walk, this godly mother slipped out of bed and crawled across the room on her hands and knees to her son's cradle. Holding the infant in her arms, she prayed that God would

22

save him and call him to preach. Until she died, this was her prayer and the prayer of his preacher father as well.

Samuel had that kind of mother. Childless, Hannah took her burden to God: "And she was in bitterness of soul, and prayed unto the Lord, and wept sore" (1:10); verse 20 adds: "She bare a son, and called his name Samuel, saying, Because I have asked him of the Lord."

Prayer that rises from a burdened heart.—Hannah's prayer for a son was a burdened prayer: "But the Lord had shut up her womb" (v. 5); "And she was in bitterness of soul, and prayed unto the Lord, and wept sore. And she vowed a vow, and said, O Lord of hosts, if thou wilt indeed look on the affliction of thine hand-maid, and remember me, and not forget thine handmaid, but wilt give unto thine handmaid a man child, then I will give him unto the Lord all the days of his life, and there shall no razor come upon his head" (vv. 10-11).

Prayer that rises from a grateful heart.—After Hannah's prayer was heard and Samuel was born, she didn't forget to thank God: "For this child I prayed; and the Lord hath given me my petition which I asked of him" (v. 27). (See Hannah's Magnificat in 1 Sam. 2:1-11.)

James A. Garfield, the twentieth president of the United States, apparently owed much to his praying mother. Miraculously saved from almost certain death by drowning one dark night in 1847, young Garfield felt his life had been saved by Divine Providence and for a special purpose. Leaving his job on the *Evening Star,* a canal boat, he returned home to Ohio. When he walked in the door, he found his mother down on her knees, praying for him by name. He told his mother he had decided to continue his education and make something of himself.[1]

Magnificent in Faith

James Barrie, best remembered for having written *Peter Pan,* has a chapter in his *Margaret Ogilvie* titled, "How My Mother Got Her Soft Face." One day Barrie's mother received a telegram telling her that her oldest son had been killed. Barrie said that his mother, a woman of strong Christian faith, never got over the sorrow. And that, Barrie said, was "how my mother got her soft face."

Hannah was such a woman. With strong, unfailing faith, she took her petition for a son to God (vv. 9-20).

Faith that takes hold on God's promises.—Burdened for a son, Hannah took hold on God and refused to let go: "Then Eli answered and said, Go in peace: and the God of Israel grant thee thy petition that thou has asked of him. And she said, let thine handmaid find grace in thy sight. So the woman went her way, and did eat, and her countenance was no more sad" (vv. 17-18).

Faith that trusts in God's leadership.—Hannah prayed and got her answer. She trusted the son promised to her to the leadership of God: "If thou wilt indeed look on the affliction of thine handmaid, and remember me, and not forget thine handmaid, but wilt give unto thy handmaid a man child, then I will give him unto the Lord all the days of his life" (v. 11). She then fulfilled her vow: "Therefore also I have lent him to the Lord; as long as he liveth he shall be lent to the Lord" (v. 28).

"Sir Wilfred Grenfell, the great Labrador missionary doctor, wrote a little book titled, 'What Christ Means to Me,' and on the 6th page he wrote these words, 'Christ meant a mother who brought Him right into our family life just by doing daily what He would do in her place.' That is what Christ meant to him—a mother who brought Christ down out of theory into every-day life, who revealed His spirit in her own personality, who never faltered in her expression of His love and mercy and tenderness and thoughtfulness."[2]

Magnificient in Love

Clarence Macartney writes: "An officer of the Confederate army tells in his 'Recollections' of how, on his way home after the sunset at Appomattox, he saw, sitting in the seat across from him, a frail, withered, hard-worked woman dressed in faded calico, with a sunbonnet on her head. She held by the hand a young man who had lost his sight from a wound received in battle. Not only was the light of the eye quenched—the light of the mind was also quenched. From her home away down in Texas the mother had come to Virginia to take her now sightless and idiotic boy back home. She had sent him forth full of energy and hope and enthusiasm. And the war had returned to her—a sightless idiot. But he was her son.

"A noble example, that, of the mother's love that many waters cannot quench, neither can the floods drown!"[3] Hannah's love for her little son, whom she gave up to God at a tender age, was no less than that.

Love that arranges priorities.—Hannah had her priorities straight. She wanted a child (v. 5); she prayed for a son (v. 10); she promised him to the Lord (v. 11); she gave him to the Lord (1:27-28; 2:1-10).

Love that never gives up.—Even in years after she gave Samuel to the Lord, Hannah continued to visit him regularly, doing for him what a mother could do (2:18-19).

Dr. Gaston Foote, a Methodist minister in Fort Worth, Texas, once told me about an experience he had the first year he was out of the seminary. As he walked down the board sidewalk of a west Texas town where he was serving the Methodist Church, he saw the bloodied body of a young man whose mother was a member of Foote's church. Picking up the unconscious young fellow, Foote carried the boy to his mother's home where she had Foote place the boy on the bed. Asking the preacher to go to the kitchen for a basin of water and some rags, the young preacher obeyed. When he returned, he saw the mother sitting on the bed with her drunken son's head in her lap. Her snow-white apron was turning crimson from the blood oozing from the boy's wounds, and the mother was stroking his hair out of his eyes and weeping audibly, "You never will let me love you when you're sober."

Magnificent in Influence

Samuel never got away from Hannah's influence. A prophet of God, and the last judge of Israel, he was one of the greatest characters of Israel's history. According to Russell Bradley Jones, "He probably lived from about 1090 to 1015 B.C." He was the greatest biblical character between Moses and David. Hannah's influence lived on in Samuel and in others touched by him.

Influence that honors God.—Hannah's influence on young Samuel set his sails in the right direction. Believing in God as a child

(3:1-10), he served God all of his days. His mother's influence taught Samuel to honor God.

Dr. George W. Truett, pastor of First Baptist Church, Dallas, Texas, for nearly fifty years, was greatly influenced by his devout mother, Mary Rebecca Truett. For twenty-six years she prayed for the conversion of her husband, Charlie. And after the father was saved, she prayed for the salvation of her children and her prayers were answered. When Dr. Lee Scarborough preached in the Truett's home church in Whitewright, Texas, he asked the people in the congregation to go around and shake hands with the person who had led them to Jesus. And Scarborough said he saw more than twenty people go "to one simple, plainly dressed woman"—the mother of George Truett.

Young Truett was saved in a Sunday night revival meeting service when he was nineteen. On the following Wednesday night, the pastor asked young Truett to testify and exhort others to come to Christ. Truett said he "was fairly carried away with a passionate concern for the salvation of that congregation" and spoke at some length. Humiliated because he had made "a spectacle" of himself, he sat down as soon as the service ended and then rushed home and went to bed. When his father and mother came home from the service, she found him in bed and he confessed how humiliated and ashamed he felt. "And my mother gently kissed me and said, 'my boy, all that is the temptation of Satan, to silence you as a witness for Christ.' And then she added these words: 'I doubt if ever in all your after life you will give a more effective testimony for Christ than you gave tonight.' Oh, marvelous encouragement from my blessed Christian mother!"[4]

Influence that blesses mankind.—Hannah mightily influenced her son and Samuel mightily influenced Israel.

George Washington's mother taught him the biblical ideals he kept before the nation. Twice each day the Bible was read and family prayers were held in his childhood home. William E. Gladstone's mother led him to faith in Christ when he was only nine. "All I think, all I write, all I am is based on the divinity of Jesus Christ," he wrote. Oliver Cromwell's mother taught him the Scriptures, and he chose as his favorite verse, "I can do all things through Christ which strengtheneth me" (Phil 4:13). Evangelist

Dwight L. Moody's mother taught him the importance of eternal values and Moody was saved at seventeen. William Penn's mother taught him the importance of faith in Christ, and he took as his motto, "This is the victory that overcometh the world, even our faith." Sir Isaac Newton's mother prayed for him every day of her life. She died when Newton was only seven, but Newton later said, "I was born in a home of godliness and dedicated to God in my infancy." Abraham Lincoln said in later life, "All that I am, all that I ever hope to be, I owe to my angel mother."

Conclusion

In his book *Hastings' Illustrations*, Robert J. Hastings told about the late F. Townley Lord who was president of the Baptist World Alliance from 1950 to 1955. A longtime pastor of London's Bloomsbury Baptist Church, Lord was also editor of *The Baptist Times*. Lord describes his father as a devout Christian, a simple working man. But about his mother he wrote: "She knew nothing of the discussions of the scholars about the Saviour as a historic figure, but everything of him as a daily Presence."[5]

That kind of mother is magnificent in the truest sense of the word.

Notes

1. See the author's book, *Living Illustrations* (Nashville: Broadman Press, 1985), pp. 114-115 for the full illustration.

2. Herbert V. Prochnow, *Speaker's Source Book of Stories, Illustrations, Epigrams and Quotations* (Grand Rapids: Baker Book House, 1955), p. 70.

3. Clarence Macartney, *Macartney's Illustrations* (New York/Nashville: Abingdon-Cokesbury Press, Copyright MCMXLV), p. 244.

4. Powhatan W. James, *George W. Truett* (Nashville: Broadman Press, 1939, 1945), p. 26.

5. Robert J. Hastings, *Hastings' Illustrations* (Nashville: Broadman Press, 1971), p. 103.

A Christian Home

Scripture: Genesis 2:18-25

Introduction

On a gray October day in 1822, a lonely, homesick, despondent man sat in his hotel room in Paris. He was far from family, friends, and his childhood home.

As he looked out his hotel window that bleak day, he saw happy parents and children having a good time. Quickly, his mind raced back across the years and across the ocean to his happy childhood days in New York. Sadly, he thought to himself, *Home sweet home. There's no place like home.*

His name was John Howard Payne. Turning away from the window through which he had been watching the children, he sat down at the desk and wrote one of the best-known and most-loved songs in American literature. It is titled, "Home, Sweet Home."

> Mid pleasures and palaces
>   Though we may roam,
> Be it ever so humble,
>   There's no place like home;
> A charm from the skies
>   Seems to hallow us there,
> Which sought through the world,
>   Is ne'er met with elsewhere.

Nothing in the world is as sweet as home. And, on this Christian Home Sunday, we turn our attention to consider the blessings and advantages of a Christian home.

The Sacredness of the Home

God established only two institutions: the home and the church. And chronologically, He first created the home.

Created by God.—After God had created Adam, He said: "It is not good that the man should be alone; I will make him an help meet for him" (Gen. 2:18). When Adam waked from his sleep, he looked at his companion and said, "This is now bone of my bones; and flesh of my flesh; she shall be called Woman, because she was taken out of Man" (v. 23). English poet laureate Alfred Tennyson once said about his wife: "The peace of God came into my life before the altar when I wedded her."

Blessed by Jesus.—The Gospels have many vignettes of Jesus in the home of His friends, blessing those homes with His presence. He was nurtured in the home of Joseph and Mary; attended the wedding in the home of unnamed friends at Cana; healed Peter's mother-in-law in Peter's home; raised Jairus's twelve-year-old daughter in Jairus's home; visited Martha and Mary in their home when Lazarus died; and was anointed by Mary in the home of Simon the Pharisee. And, by faith, we invite Him into our homes where He lifts, enobles, and blesses them.

R. L. Middleton, in his book *The Accents of Life,* told about a businessman who came home one day and was told by his wife that the new pastor had visited in their home that afternoon. When the husband asked his wife what the pastor had to say, she replied: "He asked me if Jesus dwelt in our home."

"And what did you say?" her husband asked. And she replied that she could not give an answer. Her impatient husband then asked if she told the pastor they were the largest givers in the church and that they attended services nearly every Sunday morning.

"No," his wife replied, "he did not ask me any of those questions. What he wanted to know was did Jesus live in our home."

Honored by men.—The home is not honored when couples live together and beget children outside of marriage. America's divorce rate does not honor the home. Rampant child abuse in the home does not honor it. Drunkenness in the home does not honor it.

The Purpose of the Home

In his book *Shields of Brass,* C. Roy Angell refers to novelist Scott Fitzgerald, who had just died. "On his desk was found a plot for a new novel. He was going to write a book in which a wealthy man died and left a strange will. The will bequeathed all of his millions to be divided equally, share and share alike, to all his relatives. There was one condition. They were to come and live together in his spacious mansion. Below the outlined plot was a note, 'This could be a little spot of hell.' "[1] But if a family will keep before it the divine purpose for the home, it can be a little spot of heaven.

Provide companionship.—"Therefore shall a man leave his father and his mother, and shall cleave unto his wife: and they shall be one flesh. And they were both naked, the man and his wife, and were not ashamed" (Gen. 2:24-25).

Noted Swiss psychiatrist Paul Tournier said that loneliness is "the most devastating malady of the age." And evangelist Billy Graham says that he believes the one problem that bothers more people today than any other is the problem of loneliness. More than 80 percent of psychiatric patients interviewed several years ago admitted that loneliness was the main reason they sought help. But the Christian home provides a warm companionship that addresses mankind's loneliness. God said about Adam's loneliness, "But for Adam there was not found an help meet for him" (v. 20). Addressing Adam's loneliness, God created Eve and gave her to Adam.

Beget children.—"And God blessed them and God said unto them, be fruitful, and multiply, and replenish the earth" (Gen. 1:28). Christian parents, if it is the will of God, ought to have children, teach them the ways of Jesus, and send them out into life as leaven. But just as a Christian couple has the responsibility to have children for Christ's sake, so they have the responsibility not to have more children than for whom they can provide.

Mold character.—Adam and Eve could have set a better example for their boys. Molding the character of children is one of the chief functions of a Christian home. Who of us can ever tell what the influence of godly parents has meant to us in molding our character?

Margaret T. Applegarts writes about how birth notices are eloquently paraphrased in Madagascar: " 'We have the honor to announce that Mrs. Y lives anew.' For, as the French say: 'It is the men who make the roads, but it is the women who teach the children to walk on them'; to which the Chinese could add: 'When the child goes away from home, it carries away the mother's hand.' "[2]

A man once told noted English poet Samuel Taylor Coleridge that he didn't believe in giving children any religious instructions. The man said he didn't want his child's mind to be bent in one direction or the other; he wanted him to make up his own mind.

Coleridge then invited the man to go outside with him and look at his garden, in which only weeds were growing. Surprised at the condition of the garden, the man said to Coleridge: "Why, this is not a garden! There is nothing growing here but weeds."

Coleridge responded that he did not want anything to influence his garden in any way. "I was just giving the garden a chance to express itself and to choose its own production," he told his visitor.

Conclusion

Clyde E. Fant, Jr. and William M. Pinson, Jr., in their *20 Centuries of Great Preaching,* tell about the conversion of United States Supreme Court Justice John McLean of Ohio. McLean was one of two justices who courageously voted against slavery in the noted Dred Scott Case of 1857.

McLean was not a Christian and one day, after hearing a sermon on the death of Jesus, McLean was gloriously saved. Rushing home, he announced, "I have just found that Jesus died on the cross for me. Let us go to the drawing-room and pray together." And as several attorneys waited in the room to consult McLean, the justice stated: "I have given myself to Jesus, and now I propose to invite him to my house." Addressing the assembled lawyers, he continued: "You may do as you please, stay or go; but I want Christ in this house, and now I am to make my first prayer in my own house." The lawyers remained and from that day forward McLean courageously stood for Jesus and lived the Christian life.

That's what makes a home Christian. And that's what America desperately needs.

Notes

1. C. Roy Angell, *Shields of Brass* (Broadman Press, Nashville, 1965), p. 26.

2. Margaret T. Applegarts, *Men as Trees Walking* (New York: Harper and Row Publishers, 1952), p. 130.

3. Clyde E. Fant, Jr., and William M. Pinson, Jr., *20 Centuries of Great Preaching*, Volume XI (Waco: Word Books Publishers, 1971), p. 18.

Lest We Forget

Scripture: Joshua 4:1-9

Introduction

Gaius Plinius Secundus, better known in history as Pliny the Elder, was born in AD 23 and died in AD 79, in the eruption of Mount Vesuvius. A lawyer, historian, and writer, Pliny is best remembered for his thirty-seven-volume natural history which survives.

When Italy's Mount Vesuvius began to erupt in AD 79, Pliny was the admiral of a Roman fleet anchored near Pompeii. When the billowing black smoke and ashes began to descend on Pompeii and Herculaneum, Pliny's friends urged him to flee for his life. But Pliny refused, staying in the devastated area to help the fleeing refugees.

The distant rumblings of Vesuvius did not concern Pliny. He was not anxious for his own welfare. Though his friends urged him to flee, Pliny continued to reply: "It will be all right. It will be all right. It will be all right."

But it wasn't all right. If Pliny had listened to the frantic concern of his friends, he would have survived. But, thinking everything would be all right, Pliny stayed in Pompeii and was entombed in the molten lava that flowed down the sides of the rumbling mountain.

All over America today, people are cooing the same complacent refrain: "It will be all right. It will be all right." But, I seriously wonder, will it be all right?

With crime in America burgeoning everywhere, with hard drugs deadening the minds of our young people, with the drinking of alcoholic beverages dulling the senses of our people, and with political corruption running rampant, the serious observer who loves America must ask the question, "Will it be all right?"

On this Memorial Day weekend let us review our nation's history, heritage, and hope, lest we forget who we are and the price that has been paid to keep us free.

The history of Israel gives us some guidance in this quest. Moses had died. Joshua was at Israel's helm. After wandering thirty-eight years in the wilderness, Israel had crossed the Jordan River into the Promised Land. Now, to point future generations back to the goodness of God that had spared the nation and guided them into the Land of Promise, the Lord commanded Joshua to select twelve stones, representing the twelve tribes of Israel, and build a memorial from them. The reason for the memorial is clearly stated in verses 6-7: "That this may be a sign among you, that when your children ask their fathers in time to come, saying, What mean ye by these stones? Then ye shall answer them, That the waters of Jordan were cut off before the ark of the covenant of the Lord; when it passed over Jordan, the waters of Jordan were cut off: and these stones shall be for a memorial unto the children of Israel for ever."

Israel had her memorials—numerous memorials as is attested to by the Old Testament. These memorials, including this significant memorial at Gilgal, were erected by the people to remind them of who they were, where they had been, where they were going, and what Yahweh had planned for them.

On this Memorial Day weekend, let us profit from Israel's example and take another look at America's history, heritage, and hope.

On Memorial Day we:

Mark Our History

He was a well-known Washington lawyer. In September 1814, from his vantage point on a prisoner-exchange ship, he watched the British fleet bombard Baltimore's Fort McHenry. All through the night he watched his fellow citizens on shore bear the brunt of the British attack. And the next morning, seeing that the flag was still there, he wrote a poem. But not until 1931 was his poem adopted as our national anthem:

> O say, can you see, by the dawn's early light,
> What so proudly we hailed at the twilight's last gleaming?

Whose broad stripes and bright stars, thro' the perilous fight,
O'er the ramparts we watch'd, were so gallantly streaming!
And the rockets' red glare, the bombs bursting in air
Gave proof thro' the night that our flag was still there.
O say, does that Star-Spangled Banner yet wave
O'er the land of the free and the home of the brave?

His name was Francis Scott Key. Although he intended to become an Episcopal clergyman, Key never became a man of the cloth. But he did give birth to America's most sacred hymn.

Key is buried at Frederick, Maryland, and the American flag floats reverently over his grave. Every Memorial Day a new flag is raised above Key's grave. That flag and the grounds above which it waves are a memorial held dear by Key's fellow countrymen.

As these twelve sacred stones at Gilgal were a memorial to Israel's striking history, so the scores of national monuments that dot our land are memorials to our history.

One of the most famous memorials to our history is the Liberty Bell now displayed on the first floor of the Old State House (now Independence Hall) in Philadelphia. In those hallowed halls, the second Continential Congress met in May 1775 and chose George Washington as commander-in-chief of the Continental Army. There, on July 4, 1776, John Hancock signed the Declaration of Independence.

The Liberty Bell was cast in England in 1752—twenty-four years before the Declaration of Independence was signed. Carved around the top of the bell is a passage from Leviticus 25:10 that expressed the desire of the colonists for freedom: "Proclaim liberty throughout all the land unto all the inhabitants thereof."

Weighing 2,080 pounds, the bell was first rung on July 8, 1776, to announce to Philadelphians that the Declaration of Independence had been signed. It broke as it was being rung after its arrival and in 1783 it was recast in Philadelphia from the same metal. Every July 8 until 1835 it was rung, until it cracked as it was tolling the funeral dirge for Chief Justice John Marshall.

It is no longer rung on a regular basis, but on special occasions it is struck. When the allied forces landed in France on June 6, 1944, the bell was struck and the sound was amplified by radio all over the United States.

Our history is too long and glorious to be recounted on these pages. But America's history is written in the blood of her patriots who fell in battle from Lexington to Vietnam.

What price has been paid for our freedom? In the Revolutionary War, 4,435 died; in the War of 1812, 2,260 died; in the Mexican War, 13,282 died; in the Civil War, 529,332 died; in the Spanish-American War, 2,446 died; in World War I, 116,563 died; in World War II, 407,828 died; in the Korean War, 54,246 died; and in the Vietnam War, 56,237 died.

The Battle of Concord was the second battle of the Revolutionary War. The monument erected there in 1886, along with the hymn "Concord Hymn," written for that occasion by Ralph Waldo Emerson, epitomizes our grand and glorious history:

> By the rude bridge that arched the flood,
>   Their flag to April's breeze unfurled,
> Here once the embattled farmers stood,
>   And fired the shot heard round the world.
>
> The foe long since in silence slept;
>   Alike the conqueror silent sleeps;
> And Time the ruined bridge has swept
>   Down the dark stream which seaward creeps.
>
> On this green bank, by this soft stream,
>   We set today a votive stone;
> That memory may their deed redeem,
>   When, like our sires, our sons are gone.
>
> Spirit, that made those heroes dare
>   To die, and leave their children free,
> Bid Time and Nature gently spare
>   The shaft we raise to them and thee.

Carl Sandburg relates that on one occasion he looked at the Capitol in Washington against the midnight sky, and beyond that he saw the Washington Monument towering in its magnificent splendor. Beyond that he saw the Lincoln Memorial and close by Arlington National Cemetery. Deeply moved by what he saw and felt, Sandburg exclaimed, "There is something there that men die for!"

On Memorial Day, also, we:

Mark Our Heritage

America was born in a livery stable in Philadelphia. Describing the events of that day, Thomas Jefferson, the author of the Declaration of Independence, wrote: "The weather was oppressively warm. The room occupied by the delegates was hard by a livery stable . . . the horse-flies swarmed thick and fierce, alighting on the legs of the members and biting hard through their thin silk stockings. Handkerchiefs in hand they lashed at the hungry pests to no avail."[1]

The Declaration was signed on July 4, 1776, but nearly a month earlier delegate Richard Henry Lee from Virginia had introduced a resolution: "That these United Colonies are, and of right ought to be, free and independent States, that they are absolved from all allegiance to the British crown, that all political connection between them and the state of Great Britain is, and ought to be, totally dissolved."[2]

What kind of men were these fifty-six who signed this document which William E. Gladstone called the "greatest document ever struck from the human brain"?

They were not rabble-rousers. Rather, they were men of means, education, and security but they wanted liberty. To each other they made the firm commitment, "With a firm reliance on the protection of Divine Providence, we mutually pledge to each other, our Lives, our Fortunes, and our sacred Honor."

To list all the names of the signers would require too much space. But of those fifty-six who signed the Declaration on Aug. 7, 1776, fifty were members of Congress. Six other patriots signed later.

But of those signers, most paid a high price for their patriotism. Five were captured by the British as traitors and tortured before they died. Twelve had their homes ransacked and burned. Two lost sons in the Revolutionary War. Another had two sons captured. Nine of them died from wounds or hardships of the war.

Rabble-rousers? No! Twenty-four were lawyers or judges. And nine owned large plantations. Among them was Virginian Carter Braxton, a wealthy planter. His ships were driven from the Atlantic by the British Navy and he had to sell everything to pay his debts. Braxton died poverty-stricken.

Another signer was Thomas Nelson Jr., whose home was taken over by British General Cornwallis. But Nelson urged General George Washington to fire upon Cornwallis's headquarters and, in doing so, Nelson's home was destroyed and he died bankrupt.

Francis Lewis lost his home and everything he owned. The British even put his wife in jail and she died within a few months. Also, patriot John Hart was driven from his dying wife's bedside and their thirteen children had to flee for their lives. Living in the fields and forests for more than a year, he returned home after the war to find his wife dead and his children gone. In only a few weeks Hart was dead from a broken heart.

Memorial Day marks our heritage. It reminds us where America was born and the price that was paid to birth her. Also, it strikingly reminds us of the price paid to keep us free.

When the British learned that the colonists were storing munitions at Concord, 800 redcoats were dispatched to destroy the munitions.

On the evening of April 18, 1775, Dr. Joseph Warren dispatched Paul Revere and William Dawes to warn John Hancock and Samuel Adams that the British were coming. When the British arrived at Lexington Green the following morning, they were met by Captain John Parker and forty to fifty Continental minutemen. The British were the first to open fire and when the smoke cleared, eight minutemen were dead and ten were wounded.

The British then turned toward Concord where they were attacked by the colonists, who killed three redcoats and wounded eight others. Returning to Lexington, the British troops were fired on again by the minutemen who were hidden behind rocks and trees along the road. And when the redcoats got back to Boston, 270 of their men had died but the colonists had suffered only ninety-five casualties. The die of freedom had been cast. The flag of the Continental Army had been unfurled. It was the beginning of a new nation of free men and women.

But this tells only a brief segment of our grand heritage.

Finally, on Memorial Day we ought to:

Mark Our Hope

The twelve stones were taken out of the midst of the Jordan (v. 8) and made a memorial as God commanded. It was an act of obedience and faith and a constant reminder to Israel that their hope lay in God.

So it is with America. The settlers at Jamestown recognized this when they settled these shores in 1607. One hundred and four of these hearty pioneers settled at Jamestown in the spring of 1607. But all but thirty-eight of them were dead by the time fall came. Thirteen years later, in 1620, a small band of English citizens fled from the fury of King James I. Called the Pilgrims, they settled at Plymouth. Refusing to buckle to the demands of the state church, they went into a self-imposed exile in the New World. When the Pilgrims landed at Plymouth, the forty-one men on board the Mayflower signed the "Mayflower Compact," a part of which reads: "In the name of God, Amen. . . . Having undertaken for the Glory of God, and Advancement of the Christian Faith . . . to plant the first colony in the northern Parts of Virginia . . . do . . . solemnly in the presence of God . . . covenant and combine ourselves."

When a convention was finally called to frame the Constitution of the United States, they could not agree on its contents. "After much delay, Benjamin Franklin suggested that future sessions be opened with prayer. Addressing the chair, occupied by George Washington, he said, in part, 'I have lived Sir, a long time, and the longer I live the more convincing proof I see of this truth: God governs in the affairs of men. And if a sparrow cannot fall to the ground without His notice, is it probable that an empire can rise without His aid? . . . I . . . believe that without his concurring aid we shall succeed in this political building no better than the builders of Babel.' "[3]

America's hope does not lie in her wealth, her defenses, her armament, her armies, her large budgets, or her charismatic leaders—as important as all these things are. Rather, America's hope lies in a recommitment to the spiritual values that have made her great.

It can be said of America today, as Isaiah said of Judah long ago: "The whole head is sick, and the whole heart is faint. From the sole of the foot even unto the head there is no soundness in it; but wounds, and bruises, and putrefying sores: they have not been closed, neither bound up, neither mollified with ointment" (Isa. 1:5-6).

Well did Secretary of the Treasury Salmon P. Chase express it in 1861: "No nation can be strong except in the strength of God or safe except in his defence."

And our first President, George Washington, when he took the oath of office and gave his first inaugural address on April 30, 1789, struck at the very heart of America's hope when he said: "It would be peculiarly improper to omit in this first official act, my fervent supplication to that Almighty Being who rules over the universe, who presides in the councils of the universe."

Continuing, Washington said: "No people can be bound to acknowledge and adore the invisible hand which conducts the affairs of men more than those of the United States."

Conclusion

On this Memorial Day weekend, lest we forget, we need to remember the words of Rudyard Kipling:

> God of our fathers, known of old,
>   Lord of our farflung battle line,
> Beneath whose awful hand we hold
>   Dominion over palm and pine:
> Lord God of Hosts, be with us yet,
>   Lest we forget—lest we forget!
>
> The tumult and the shouting dies,
>   The captains and the kings depart.
> Still stands Thine ancient sacrifice,
>   An humble and a contrite heart.
> Lord God of Hosts, be with us yet,
>   Lest we forget—lest we forget!

Notes

1. R. L. Middleton, *My Cup Runneth Over* (Nashville: Broadman Press, 1960), pp. 69-70.

2. Ibid, p. 69.

3. Virginia Ely, *Devotions for Personal and Group Worship* (Old Tappan, N.J.: Fleming H. Revell Co., 1960), pp. 79-80.

Marks of a Godly Father

Scripture: Genesis 22:1-19

Introduction

We have been told that figures don't lie. But sometimes they do.

For example, in a sermon Dr. Harry Emerson Fosdick said that some chemists had figured out what the average man is worth. He contains enough fat to make seven bars of soap; enough iron to make a medium-sized nail; enough magnesium for one good dose of magnesia; enough potassium and sulfur to create a small explosion; enough lime to whitewash a small chicken coop; enough sugar to fill a shaker; and enough potassium to make 2,200 match tips. Fosdick said the chemists figured at the rates which were then current that a man was worth about ninety-eight cents.

But in his book *Sermons from the Mount*, Charles M. Crowe says that the 150-pound, ninety-eight-cent man is now worth $85.5 billion. Crowe said researchers believe that the atoms in a 150-pound man have an energy potential of 11.4 killowatt hours per pound—$570 million per pound! Total value—$85.5 billion.

I don't know about all this, but I do know that a godly father is worth more than can ever be told. I know that, because I had one.

On this Father's Day occasion, we will look at an experience out of the life of Abraham, "The friend of God," and by so doing we shall discern certain marks that a godly father possesses.

Marked by Faithful Obedience

God told Abraham: "Take now thy son, thine only son Isaac, whom thou lovest, and get thee into the land of Moriah; and offer him there for a burnt offering upon one of the mountains which I will tell thee of" (v. 2). And without hesitating, Abraham obeyed: "And they came to the place which God had told him of; and Abraham built an altar there, and laid the wood in order, and

bound Isaac his son, and laid him on the altar upon the wood. And
Abraham streched forth his hand, and took the knife to slay his
son" (vv. 9-10). Although it is difficult for us to understand why
God gave Abraham such a command, Abraham's obedience is
obvious.

Scottish physician Sir James Simpson (1811-1870) specialized in
obstetrics. In 1847 Simpson discovered that chloroform was a good
substitute for ether. Although much debate followed Simpson's
announcement, when he delivered Prince Leopold, the seventh
child of Queen Victoria, using chloroform, the debate ended. In
an Edinburgh cemetery, one will find the grave of Simpson's little
daughter, and on the grave is the epitaph, "Nevertheless, I live."

Last words are important. John Wesley's last words were, "The
best of all, God is with us." George Washington's last words were,
"It is well, I die hard, but I'm not afraid to go." And the last words
of Ibsen, the Norwegian dramatist, were "Nevertheless." And in
Gethsemane, Jesus wept, "Nevertheless. . . ." The first and last
word of a godly father, in all his decisions, ought to be "Nevertheless, thy will be done."

Marked by Straight Priorities

Abraham had his priorities straight.

"And Abraham said unto his young men, abide ye here with the
ass; and I and the lad will go yonder and worship, and come again
unto you" (v. 5). Facing his son's death, Abraham went to Moriah
to worship. He could have fled from God as Jonah tried to do, but
he had his priorities straight. He worshiped when he could have
rebelled.

Dr. Gaston Foote, former pastor of First Methodist Church, Fort
Worth, Texas, tells in his book *Living in Four Dimensions*, about
going to a small town in Indiana for a speaking engagement. He
got off in too big a hurry and forgot his razor, so he had to go to
the barbershop and get a shave. It was an old shop, run by an old
barber who had been there for thirty years. As they talked, Foote
remarked that life must be pretty dull in such a small town, adding
that folks probably went to Chicago pretty often to celebrate. The
old barber agreed that things were pretty dull and a good many
of the town's citizens did go to Chicago to celebrate, but he said

that he didn't go because "I've got to be good. I have four fine sons at my house." It seems that the old barber had his priorities straight.

In a cemetery in Scotland, there is a stone marker on which the following epitaph is written: "He was _____; He was what? Think of what a man should be; he was that."

Look at another mark of a godly father:

Marked by Simple Trust

When Isaac asked Abraham where the sacrifice for the offering was, Abraham replied: "My son, God will provide himself a lamb for a burnt offering: so they went both of them together" (v. 8). Isaac was Abraham and Sarah's only son and Abraham knew that through Isaac God had promised to bless mankind. But there is no hint in the passage that Abraham questioned God as to how he could possibly do that if Isaac was slain. As was the habit of his life, Abraham trusted God to work all that out.

Alexander the Great was ill and his doctor came daily to give him medicine. One day, after Alexander had received a letter accusing the doctor of trying to poison him, the doctor came in, gave Alexander the medicine, and Alexander took it. He then handed the doctor the letter to read, showing the doctor how much he trusted him. Abraham, a godly father, demonstrates for every father who would be godly the kind of simple trust he must have in God.

In *Macartney's Illustrations*, the late Clarence Macartney wrote: "Dwight L. Moody's favorite verse was Isaiah 12:2: 'I will trust, and not be afraid.' He used to say: 'You can travel first class or second class to heaven. Second class is, 'What time I am afraid I will trust.' First class is, 'I will trust, and not be afraid.' That is the better way. Why not buy a first-class ticket?"[1]

Tennyson, in his poem "In Memoriam," wrote:

> Strong Son of God, immortal Love,
> Whom we, that have not seen thy face,
> By faith, and faith alone, embrace,
> Believing where we cannot prove.

William Wilberforce (1759-1833) spent his life fighting the slave trade in the British Empire. Losing his considerable fortune when he was seventy-one, Wilberforce had to move out of his lovely home and move in with his married sons. Two days after he learned how great his losses were, he noted in his diary: "A solitary walk with the psalmist—evening quiet." Simple trust made the difference.

A godly father is:

Marked by Tender Compassion

Can you imagine how cut to the heart Abraham was when Isaac asked: "My father: and he said, Here am I, my son. And he said, Behold the fire and the wood: but where is the lamb for a burnt offering? And Abraham said, My son, God will provide himself a lamb for a burnt offering: so they went both of them together" (vv. 7-8). Isaac, no doubt, even in his old age, remembered the tender compassion of his brokenhearted father when Abraham answered Isaac's cutting question. A godly father is marked by tender compassion.

Dr. Millard Alford Jenkens, a former pastor of First Baptist Church, Abilene, Texas, told about his father in his book *Special Day Sermons*. The elder Jenkens, clerk of the little country church the family attended, was a modest and timid man. His son said that his father was no public speaker and that his voice would falter even when he read the minutes at the Saturday business meetings of the little country church. Jenkens said he never heard his father give a talk at church or lead in public prayer and that the children wondered why their father was so timid and withdrawn.

But one evening about sunset, Jenkens related, his brother came to him and said, "I was down in the woods near the house and heard Pa praying, and he was praying for you and me." Jenkens said that what his brother told him made a deep impression on his young life and was, even in the pastor's last years, one of the sweetest memories of his boyhood.

Finally, a godly father is:

Marked by Divine Blessings

Abraham's faith was doubly blessed: Isaac was spared (Gen. 22: 11-14) and through his descendants all mankind has been blessed

(vv. 15-19). Both a godly father and his family will be blessed by the example the father sets.

G. K. Chesterton (1874-1936), an English writer, told that as a boy he had a little toy theater. One of the cardboard cutouts in the little theater was a man with a large golden key. Chesterton related that he didn't remember what character the cardboard man with the golden key represented, but that as a boy he always thought of the figure as representing his father. He did that, he said, because his father had unlocked so many marvelous doors for him.

A godly father unlocks the door to many divine blessings for his family.

Conclusion

Samuel Shoemaker (1893-1963) was an American Episcopal priest. In *20 Centuries of Great Preaching*, Fant and Pinson quote Shoemaker: "The word 'father' as applied to God must contain principally one association, i.e. one's human father. If the main content in that relationship is fear, it will carry over to God: if the main content is love, that will carry over to God. A remarkable man, Harry Hadley, was superintendent of a rescue mission which my old parish in New York ran. His father was Samuel Hadley, himself a wonderfully converted man (he is mentioned in William James's *Varieties of Religious Experience*) and superintendent of the Water Street Mission. His son was a wastrel all his father's life, and was not converted until his death; but the son often said to me, 'When I call God "Father," I don't have to make much change in its content.' Whatever else you give or fail to give to children, give them affection, lots of it. It is not inconsistent with discipline, but it greatly modifies how discipline is administered. They charge our unlovingness to God, or they are helped to believe in His perfect love by our imperfect love. This is not spoiling and doing everything they want; but it is a deep assurance of love that a child knows he can count on. 'If he cannot love, and feel love from, his human father and family whom he has seen, how can he feel it from God whom he has never seen?' "[2]

Notes

1. Clarence E. Macartney, *Macartney's Illustrations* (New York and Nashville: Abingdon-Cokesbury Press, 1945), p. 401.

2. Clyde E. Fant Jr., William M. Pinson Jr., *20 Centuries of Great Preaching, Volume XI* (Waco: Word Books, 1971), p. 79.

America at the Crossroads

Scripture: Joshua 24:14-16

Introduction

"Remember the Alamo" and "Remember Pearl Harbor" are well-known battle cries from the pages of American history. And each strengthened the resolve of patriots to fight and die for freedom.

The battle of the Alamo was fought in San Antonio, Texas, in 1836. When the Texans severed their relations with Mexico and declared themselves to be free, the Mexican government quickly responded by sending General Santa Anna and a contingent of 5,000 Mexican soldiers to the tiny Texas mission.

The seige of the Alamo began on February 23, 1836, as the mission and the 150 defenders inside its walls were attacked. At 8 A.M., on the morning of March 6, Santa Anna's men scaled the walls of the Alamo and killed the last six remaining defenders, including David Crockett, Jim Bowie, and William B. Travis.

But the defense of the Alamo was not in vain for it had given General Sam Houston time to rally an army for the cause of freedom. Retreating eastward, Houston and his men came to a fork in the road in deep southeast Texas which was marked by a gnarled, old tree known in Texas history as the "Which-way Tree."

The road to the left stretched out into the marshes of southeast Texas and Louisiana. The road to the right led to San Jacinto.

Faced with a choice, Houston took the road to the right and surprised the overconfident Mexican troops at San Jacinto on April 21. Crushing the Mexican army, Houston captured San Jacinto and a great republic was born.

Israel had come to a similar hour. She was at the crossroads—at her "Which-way Tree"—and her destiny was at stake. Moses had led the Jews out of Egypt and through the wilderness. Under

Joshua's leadership, they had marched into the Promised Land and had begun to take it. But many battles and much opposition lay ahead for Israel before Canaan would be hers.

Knowing his days were numbered, old Joshua rallied Israel and reminded her of her great heritage and called upon her to renew her faith in God. Joshua knew this was the nation's only hope.

Like the Texans at their "Which-way Tree," and like Israel standing before Joshua, America today stands at the crossroads. Our past has been positive and glorious, but today the nation is muddled and confused, and our future is uncertain. Too long moral and spiritual principles have been sacrificed on altars of pleasure and materialism. America is at the crossroads and we need divine guidance, for our survival is at stake.

As America stands at the crossroads, there are several things we ought to do:

We Ought to Review Our Blessings

Joshua did this for Israel (vv. 2-13,17). Israel hung on Joshua's every word. Their old leader reviewed the divine blessings upon them beginning with Abraham (vv. 2-3); through Isaac, Jacob, Moses, and Aaron (vv. 4-5); through the Red Sea (vv. 6-7); victories along the way (vv. 8-10); and into Canaan (vv. 11*ff.*). God had given them cities which they did not build and they had eaten from vineyards and olive trees they did not plant (vv. 12-13). It is an eloquent picture of the divine blessings that have attended their way.

It is healthy for a nation to review its blessings. America's blessings are so numerous that libraries could be written extolling them. We are blessed with natural resources, fertile lands, rich oceans, gracious people, a varied climate, and so forth. America is a masterpiece of magnificence painted by the Divine Artisan. Although we have only about 6 percent of the earth's geography, we have about 52 percent of the world's material wealth and 30 percent of its energy.

We Ought to Remember Our Heritage

Joshua's word to Israel was "remember." "Remember who you are!"

Israel had Abraham whom God called to become a mighty nation (vv. 2-3); Isaac, Jacob, and Esau (v. 4); and mighty Moses and eloquent Aaron (v. 5).

America's greatest resource is her people. A nation loses its sense of direction when it forgets its heritage. Rome had Virgil who sang of her greatness, but America had Washington who prayed a nation into being. Greece had eloquent Demosthenes who stirred her pagan soul with his eulogies, but America had Thomas Paine who prodded a nation toward freedom with his sharp pen. Macedonia had mighty Alexander with his world conquest, but America had Thomas Jefferson and the Declaration of Independence. Britain had Carlyle and Churchill whose leadership turned the tide in dark days, but America had Roger Williams, the father of religious liberty. A nation loses its moorings when it forgets its heritage. Under difficult circumstances, our forefathers labored to draft a world-shaking statement known as the Declaration of Independence.

Tom Paine wrote about our heritage. In December 1776, Washington and his men were encamped across the Delaware River from Trenton, New Jersey. The Revolution was not going well. But Tom Paine was there. "Drawing a drum between his knees, Paine wrote the first of the *Crisis* papers. Washington read it and sent a rider off to Philadelphia to have copies printed and brought back with all haste. On Christmas night, 1776, copies were distributed and read. Nat Griste, leaning to the lantern he had hung on a bough, cleared his throat and lifted his voice over the wind." Griste read Paine's words: "These are the times that try men's souls. The summer soldier and the sunshine patriot will, in this crisis, shrink from the service of their country, but he that stands it *now*, deserves the love and thanks of man and woman. Tyranny, like hell, is not easily conquered; yet we have this consolation with us, that the harder the conflict, the more glorious the triumph."[1]

That night Washington and his men crossed the Delaware, and in the cold dawn of December 26, 1776, defeated the Hessian soldiers, and turned the tide of freedom in their favor.

American historian Carl Sandburg describes his emotions one night as he viewed the Washington Monument and the Lincoln Memorial in the nation's capital. Looking also at the white crosses in Arlington National Cemetery, Sandburg exclaimed: "There is something there that men die for."

We Ought to Renew Our Faith

Israel never stood taller than on this day when she renewed her faith to the God who had made and preserved her (vv. 14-15): "And the people answered and said, God forbid that we should forsake the Lord, to serve other gods; For the Lord our God, he it is that brought us up . . . out of the land of Egypt . . . therefore will we also serve the Lord; for he is our God" (vv. 16-18).

America desperately needs a renewal of her faith in God. We never stand taller than when we are on our knees in rededication to Him. And more than we need cures for the diseases that decimate our people, we need a spiritual renewal of our faith.

In the bitter winter of 1778, Washington's cold and hungry army of only 11,000 men was encamped at Valley Forge. Many of them were too weak or too sick to fight and 3,000 of them died during those cold months.

"One day a farmer approaching the camp heard an earnest voice. On coming nearer, he saw George Washington on his knees, his cheeks wet with tears, praying to God. The farmer returned home and said to his wife: 'George Washington will succeed! George Washington will succeed! The Americans will secure their independence!'

" 'What makes you think so, Isaac?' asked his wife.

"The farmer replied: 'I heard him pray, Hannah, out in the woods today, and the Lord will surely hear his prayer. He will Hannah; thee may rest assured He will.' "[2]

And he did!

Today Americans use the right vocabulary in worship; piously sing the great hymns of the faith; have Bibles in their homes; and eloquent preachers in their pulpits. We have a form of godliness, but deny God's lordship over us.

On the Lord's Day, His house is forsaken for the lake, the highway, the summer cottage, and the sports arena. We pray little except in crisis situations. We steal God's tithe money and build for ourselves houses of clay and lives of straw. We get much only to lose everything!

Until we renew our faith in God, we will continue to grope down dark highways, talking much about peace but never finding it. Our problems are more spiritual than economic and godlessness is the national termite eating away our soul. And this is one thing out of which we cannot buy our way! Repentance and renewed faith is our only hope.

Conclusion

Never were words of patriotism more eloquently written than those penned by Scotsman Sir Walter Scott in *The Lay of the Last Minstrel.*

> Breathes there the man with soul so dead,
> Who never to himself hath said,
>   This is my own, my native land!
> Whose heart hath ne'er within him burn'd,
> As home his footsteps he hath turn'd,
>   From wandering on a foreign strand?
> If such there breathe, go, mark him well;
> For him no Minstrel raptures swell;
> High though his titles, proud his name,
> Boundless his wealth as wish can claim;
> Despite those titles, power, and pelf,
> The wretch, concentred all in self,
> Living, shall forfeit fair renown,
> And, doubly dying, shall go down
> To the vile dust, from whence he sprung,
> Unwept, unhonor'd, and unsung.

Notes

1. Lewis L. Dunnington, *Power to Become* (New York: The Macmillan Co., 1956), pp. 94-95.

2. Walter B. Knight, *Knight's Master Book of New Illustrations* (Grand Rapids: Wm. B. Erdmans Publishing Co., 1956), p. 461.

Christ's Compassion
for the World

Scripture: Matthew 9:35-38

Introduction

As a young man, David Livingstone heard Dr. Robert Moffat speak about the need for missionaries in Africa. Later, in a personal conference with Moffat, Livingstone asked, "Sir, do you think I would do as a missionary to Africa?"

Encouraged by Moffat, Livingstone took his medical degree in 1840 and sailed for Africa. Thirty-three years later, April 30, 1873, Livingstone died in Africa at Lake Bangweulu.

On the evening of November 16, 1840, preparing to sail for Africa, Livingstone went to his parents' home to tell them good-bye. Sitting up all night, they talked about things that were close to their hearts. At 5 AM the following morning, they had breakfast, knelt for family prayers, and young Livingstone read from Psalms 121 and 135. Then young Livingstone and his father walked to Glasgow, said good-bye, and parted, never to meet again on this earth.

Arriving in Africa, Livingstone worked for a while at a mission station, but then pushed 700 miles inland to Dr. Moffat's station. One day an old chief said to Livingstone, "I wish you would give me medicine to change my heart. It is proud and angry always." Livingstone then showed the old heathen the way to Jesus.

On the morning of April 30, 1873, Livingstone's African servants entered his hut and found the sixty-year-old missionary dead on his knees. Removing his heart, they buried it beneath a tree and carried his body on their shoulders 900 miles to the coast—a journey that took nine months. And today, the visitor to London's Westminster Abbey will see in the floor at the entrance to the Abbey, the grave of one of the greatest Christian missionaries in history.

What was it that caused David Livingstone to turn his back on a bright future in Scotland to serve Jesus, living and dying in Africa? Why, the question is simple to answer: Livingstone shared Christ's compassion for a needy world and followed the steps of his Savior to where the needs were the greatest.

In this Scripture we have three clear, powerful statements that reveal Christ's compassion for our needy world.

What Jesus Sees

"But when he saw the multitudes" (v. 36*a*).

He sees the world's physical needs.—Christ's ministry was three-fold: teaching, preaching, and healing. His seeing the physical needs of the people is described in verse 35: "and healing every sickness and every disease among the people."

James warns: "If a brother or sister be naked, and destitute of daily food, and one of you say unto them, Depart in peace, be warmed and filled; notwithstanding ye give them not those things which are needful to the body; what doth it profit?" (Jas. 2:15-16). Jesus ministered to the physical needs of the people: He fed the multitude; healed the lepers; raised Lazarus, and so forth.

He sees the world's spiritual needs.—"And Jesus went about . . . preaching the gospel of the kingdom" (v. 35*a*). Their spiritual needs are also described in verse 36: "fainted"; "scattered abroad"; "sheep having no shepherd." "Fainted" means habitual distress. Vincent said: to "flay, rend, or mangle." In relationship to sheep, as it is used here, Vincent said: "It might be rendered here 'fleeced.'" Vincent says "scattered" means "to throw (prostrate) or cast." It describes inner dejection, weariness. Robertson said these words describe "Their religious condition. . . . Bewildered by those who should have taught them; hindered from entering into the kingdom of heaven." Nicoll says "scattered" describes sheep unable to go a step further. "A flock can get into such a condition only when it has no shepherd to care for it and guide it to the pastures."

Clarence Macartney tells about a man in Germany who, many years ago, was working on a church steeple. Losing his footing, he was falling to certain death when he fell on a lamb that was grazing in the churchyard. The lamb died, but the man was saved by the lamb! In gratitude he had carved over the doorway of the church the picture of a lamb. But millions of fainting, scattered, shepherdless sheep have never heard the good news that they can be saved by the blood of the Lamb (John 1:29).

What Jesus Feels

"He was moved with compassion on them" (v. 36*b*).

Jesus feels compassion—"Compassion" means pity. It is not a nostalgic, feminine emotion reserved only for tenderhearted ladies. Christ's pity for the people, according to the Greek grammar, was sudden, immediate, full, overflowing, and moved Him deeply.

During the four-year long Civil War, 400 men died each day. And the tragedy of that war left a scar on the United States that has not healed. When President Abraham Lincoln was told that Richmond, the capital of the Confederacy, was about to surrender, he went from Washington to Virginia. Entering the office of Jefferson Davis, the president of the Confederacy, Lincoln asked to be left alone. But his aides became anxious about Lincoln after he had been in Davis's office for more than two hours. Gently opening the door, they looked in to see the compassionate President sitting in Jefferson Davis's chair. Lincoln's head was resting on his hands and his body shaking with sobs. Perhaps Lincoln was America's most compassionate President. But his pity for nearly 600,000 men who had died in the war can never compare to the pity Jesus feels for the world that is at war against Him.

Why Jesus feels compassion.—Robertson said: "They were harassed . . . hindered from entering into the kingdom of heaven (23:13), laden with the burdens which the Pharisees laid upon them (23:3). . . . In a state of mental dejection."[1]

Sir Edwin Landseer, a painter born in London in 1802, was a well-known English artist of that day. J. Wallace Hamilton in his book *Ride the Wild Horses*, tells how Landseer once turned a bad stain on a newly decorated wall of a hotel in Scotland into a thing of beauty.

Studying the blotch on the wall, Landseer went to work with his crayons, charcoal, and oil paints. When he had finished, he had transformed the ugly stains into majestic rocks with a tumbling cataract pouring over them. He turned the other stains into a magnificent stag, leaping into the churning torrent, pursued by hunters. The master's skillful touches turned a marred wall into a thing of beauty. And that's what Jesus Christ has done for millions of hurting people and will do for all who come to Him by faith.

What Jesus Says

Jesus says three things:

The harvest is great.—"The harvest truly is plenteous" (Matt. 9:37b); (see also John 4:31-35.) Someone has said that if there were only one true believer on earth, and that during an entire year he made one convert, then there would be two believers. If those two believers each made a convert during the next year, then there would be four. The next year those four Christians would each win one, and then there would be eight. The question was then asked how long it would take to win the entire world to Jesus, following the same pattern. At the end of thirty-five years there would be 2,147,483,648 Christians. The next year they could win that number again to Jesus. "The harvest truly is plenteous."

There are few laborers.—"But the laborers are few" (v. 37c). Nicoll says that professional laborers are abundant "but powerless to win the people because they are without sympathy, hope, and a credible, acceptable gospel."

In his book *Challenges to the Cross,* Wayne Dehoney says that Alexander the Great conquered the world with an army of 35,000; Genghis Kahn conquered it with 200,000 men; Tamerlane conquered it with 230,000; and the Communists took Russia with 40,000. What about the Christian army of ministers, Sunday School teachers, dedicated women, missionaries, and lay believers —an army sufficiently large to win the world when they decide to do so?

We must be more than spectators.—"Pray ye therefore the Lord of the harvest, that he will send forth labourers into His harvest" (v. 38). Jesus is talking about personal involvement which begins with prayer.

Consider these great Christian prayers of history: David Brainerd, early American missionary, kneeling in the snow praying for the Indians; evangelist Charles Finney wrapped in a buffalo robe, praying all night in a hayloft; evangelist Dwight L. Moody who made it a habit to rise at 4 AM each morning to pray for revival; John and Charles Wesley, along with George Whitefield, who brought revival to England and America through prayer; George Mueller who prayed sixty-three years and eight months for an unsaved friend who was converted at Mueller's funeral service; and the great American missionary enterprise spawned in the historic haystack prayer meeting. Winning our world to Christ hinges on prayer. It is the initial step of personal involvement.

William Booth left the Methodist church in England to found the Salvation Army. Author Robert Hastings tells how Booth became more than a spectator: "I hungered for Hell. I pushed into the midst of it, the East Side of London. For days I stood in the seething streets, drinking it all in and loving it all; yes, I loved it because I loved the souls that made up the muddy stream. I went home one night to my wife and said to her: 'My darling, I have given myself, I have given you, and I have given our children to the service of these souls.' "[2]

Conclusion

J. Hudson Taylor, the nineteenth-century missionary to China, first sailed for China in 1853. Although he had to return home because of illness, he could not stay at home because of his burden for the millions of unsaved people in that great land. In 1865 he founded the China Inland Mission whose sole objective was to reach China for Jesus.

On one occasion Taylor was in Hangchow, witnessing and distributing books. As he sat one night in a teahouse to rest, he saw an elderly man staring at him. The elderly man asked him if he were a foreigner and if he had books in the bag which lay on the table. He then wanted to know if Taylor was a teacher of a foreign religion. When Taylor answered "yes" to each of the questions, the old man replied that he had been seeking for the truth for many years. A few nights before their meeting, he told Taylor, a man clothed in white appeared to him and told him to go to Hangchow where he would find a foreigner, sitting at a table, with a bag of books before him. Obedient to the vision, the elderly man said he had come on several occasions but had found no person such as was described to him in his vision. Taylor led the man to Christ and he became a strong Christian.

There are millions of people outside the walls of our churches who are seeking the Savior. To reach them, we must share with Jesus His compassion for a lost world.

Notes

1. A. T. Robertson, *Word Pictures in the New Testament*, Vol. I (Nashville: Broadman Press, 1930), p. 76.

2. Robert J. Hastings, *A Word Fitly Spoken* (Nashville: Broadman Press, 1962), p. 39.

Making the Most of Life

Scripture: Acts 9:36-43

Introduction

Few have blessed us as much as did Thomas Alva Edison. Among his inventions are the electric light bulb, the motion picture machine, the telephone transmitter that paved the way for the modern telephone, the mimeograph machine, the phonograph, and the stock ticker—to mention only a few. It can be truthfully said of Edison that he made the most of what God gave him.

Nothing is more important than that. And that is the great challenge that lies before each of you young people today. When you come to the end of life and stand before God, He is going to ask, "What did you do with the life I gave you?"

In the passage of Scripture at which we are looking, there is a marvelous example of a woman named Dorcas who made the most of the life God gave her. Although she never enjoyed fame or riches, she lived nobly and successfully and left for us a worthy example to emulate.

Dorcas's example shows us three things about making the most of life.

You Must Be Something

"Now there was at Joppa a certain disciple" (v. 36a). Although Dorcas was a prominent woman at Joppa, this is the only time her name appears in the Scriptures. She never speaks a word, but the testimony of the Holy Spirit to her life is abundantly clear. He tells us what she was: "Now there was at Joppa a certain *disciple* named Tabitha, which by interpretation is called Dorcas" (v. 36, author's italics).

Dorcas was something: humble, simple, devout, a committed follower of Jesus Christ. The Bible says she was a "disciple."

What is the measure of success? It isn't money. Jay Gould, one of America's wealthiest men, said: "I suppose I am the most miserable devil on earth."

It is not fame. Lord Beaconsfield, whose real name was Benjamin Disraeli, was the only Jew ever elected prime minister of Great Britain. But this successful politician wrote: "Youth is a blunder; manhood a struggle; old age a regret."

It isn't pleasure. English author Lord Byron wrote about pleasure:

> My days are in the yellow leaf;
>   The flowers and fruits of love are gone;
> The worm, the canker, and the grief
>   Are mine alone!

It isn't power. Napoleon, the conqueror of Europe, imprisoned on the rock-bound island of Saint Helena, said: "Alexander, Caesar, Charlemagne, and myself founded empires. But on what did we found them? On force! Jesus Christ alone founded his on love, and today there are millions who would die for him."

Since one cannot build life on these things, then on what can one build it? The answer is found in the example of Dorcas: be a Christian, a disciple, a follower of Jesus Christ. Trust Him as your personal Savior, crown Him as Lord of your life. This is the first step in making the most of life.

American sculptor Lorado Taft was placing some lights around the statue of a boy sculpted by Italian sculptor Donatello. Placing the lights on the floor and shining them up into the boy's face to illuminate it, Taft observed that the boy's lighted face looked more like the face of a moron than that of a bright, young boy. Changing the lights and trying every possible arrangement, Taft finally decided to put the lights above the boy so they would shine down on his head. Taft then stepped back to look at the boy's face and it shone with a radiance of an angel.

Let the love and light of Jesus Christ shine into your mind, upon your heart, and across your face. Become a disciple of the matchless Savior and you will take the first giant step in making the most of your life.

You Must Do Something

We are told what Dorcas did: "This woman was full of good works and almsdeeds which she did" (v. 36c). Dorcas, following the example of Jesus, lived for others. "Good works" and "almsdeeds" were here trademarks.

Our Lord commended good works of this nature when He rebuked Judas for accusing Mary of wasting the perfume which she had poured over the head of Jesus: "Let her alone, why trouble ye her? she hath wrought a good work on me. For ye have the poor with you always, and whensoever ye will ye may do them good: but me ye have not always. She hath done what she could" (Mark 14: 6-8a).

Catch the last statement of Jesus: "She hath done what she could." This is the real test of successful living. When life is over and we stand before God, let Him be able to say of us that we did what we could; that we used the talents He gave to us to the best of our ability.

What we can do, though we may think it is small and unimportant, may be very important. English became the national language of the United States by only one vote. Thomas Jefferson became President of the United States, winning over Aaron Burr, by only one vote. Only four electoral votes brought Abraham Lincoln to the presidency. One electoral vote put Rutherford B. Hayes in the presidency. And that one vote cast for Hayes was cast by a senator who, himself, had been elected on the strength of only one vote. Only one vote saved President Andrew Johnson from being impeached. And only one vote brought Texas, California, Idaho, Oregon, and Washington into the Union.

There is something each of us can do to bless others and improve life. But you can't wait until you are older or wiser to begin. Daniel was only a teenager when he purposed that he would "not defile himself with . . . the king's meat" (Dan. 1:8). Joseph was only seventeen when he was sold into slavery which would eventuate in the saving of Israel. He was only thirty when he was chosen prime minister of Egypt. David was only a teenager when he slew

Goliath. Alexander the Great was only twenty when he left home to conquer the world, and only thirty-three when he did it. At twenty-four, William Pitt was the youngest prime minister of Great Britain; Napoleon was only twenty-six when he was proclaimed emperor of Paris; William Cullen Bryant wrote his immortal "Thanatopsis" when he was only sixteen; John Keats wrote "Ode on a Grecian Urn" and "Endymion" before he was twenty-six; and Joan of Arc was only sixteen when she led France to victory. Even as a young person there is a lot you can do, should do, and must do. So, get started! Do something!

You Must Leave Something

"And all the widows stood by him [Peter] weeping, and shewing the coats and garments which Dorcas made, while she was with them" (v. 39c). She left something by which she would be remembered. There is no hint in the passage that she left a large estate over which her children and others would wrangle. But she left something more worthwhile: she had spent her life living for others and what she left behind gave silent testimony to the love that motivated her.

One Christmas when William Booth, the founder of the Salvation Army, wanted to send Christmas greetings to his Christian army around the world, he had to keep his message short because funds were scarce. So he cut his greeting down to one simple word which he telegraphed to every Salvation Army worker around the world: "Others!"

This was Dorcas's priority. She lived to serve others. And this must be your priority if you would make the most of life. Live for others and leave behind a fragrance that shall long bless others.

Cain lived only for himself and his name is a byword. Herod lived only for himself and the memory of him is wretched. The pharaohs lived only for themselves and their names are inglorious. Jezebel and Ahab lived only for themselves and their names burn the tongue when spoken. Judas lived for himself and his name is despised.

There is a part of you that will never die. Your body will be laid in the grave but your influence will never die. Generations to come will rise up to bless or curse your memory.

Morse lives through every telegram that is sent. Edison lives through every light bulb that is illuminated. Bell lives through every telephone that rings. Pasteur lives through every immunization shot that is given. Priestly lives through every bottle of oxygen that is used by the sick. Galileo lives through every new star that is discovered. Eli Whitney lives through every bale of cotton that is ginned. Shakespeare lives through every student that studies literature. The Wright brothers live through every airplane that carries travelers through the sky. Jenner lives through every smallpox vaccination given. Sir James Simpson lives through every painless surgery that is performed. And Gutenberg lives through every paper, book, and Bible that is read. The good you do will never die!

Henry Wadsworth Longfellow wrote about this part of you that lives on after you are gone in "The Arrow and the Song":

> I shot an arrow into the air,
> It fell to earth, I knew not where;
> For so swiftly it flew, the sight
> Could not follow in its flight.
>
> I breathed a song into the air,
> It fell to earth, I knew not where;
> For who has sight so swift and strong
> That it can follow the flight of song?
>
> Long, long afterward in an oak
> I found the arrow still unbroke,
> And the song, from beginning to end
> I found again in the heart of a friend.

So, Dorcas is our example of making the most of life. She left us a pattern that needs no improvement: be something; do something; and leave something.

Conclusion

A. J. Cronin is one of my heroes. Born in 1896, Cronin was a British doctor who gave up his practice of medicine to write. But when he first started writing novels, he became so discouraged that he wadded up the manuscript and threw it away. No one, he thought, would want to read what he wrote.

According to Jack Gulledge in his book *Ideas and Illustrations for Inspirational Talks*, Cronin walked down a country road and saw a farmer who was plowing his field. Cronin complained about being so discouraged and that he had decided to quit writing. Giving Cronin a rather hard look, the farmer pointed at the land and told Cronin that both he and his father had worked it with little to show for their labors. But he said he kept on plowing and planting the soil, believing, as his father had believed before him, that if he plowed and sowed long enough, someday the farm would produce a rich harvest.

Cronin got the farmer's drift and went back home, took the manuscript out of the trash can, and dried it in the oven. Although he was ill, he finished the manuscript, his first novel, *Hatter's Castle*, that established him as a writer. In 1937 he produced *The Citadel;* in 1941, *The Keys of the Kingdom;* in 1950, *The Spanish Gardner;* in 1956, *A Thing of Beauty;* in 1958, *The Northern Lights;* and in 1961, *The Judas Tree.*

You will discover that nothing in this life comes easily. But some things are worth working for. By faith and grace, work to make the most of life. It's the only one you will have on this earth.

How to Bless a Child

Scripture: Mark 10:13-16

Introduction

One Sunday morning a good many years ago, a ten-year-old boy attended a special Lenten service in Pompton, New Jersey. It was a cold, rainy morning and the ten-year-old was the only one present—except for the preacher.

The boy wondered what the minister would do. But when the hour set for worship arrived, the minister walked into his pulpit in all his solemn dignity, as though the church were filled to capacity. Later, after the boy had grown to manhood, he recalled the experience: "He looked down on me with a smile of great dignity and sincerity and he commenced the service as if the church were crowded to the walls. He talked earnestly to me— and to God."[1]

When the time came for the morning offering, the minister stepped down from the pulpit and placed the offering plate on the altar railing. Reverently, the lad walked up to the altar and placed his nickel in the plate. And as he put his nickel in the offering plate, the preacher smiled at him and put a big, gentle hand on the boy's head.

Many years later, recalling that experience, the boy grown to manhood commented: "In walking back to my seat, I knew this man's God was a real God, and that his faith was God-like in its monumental simplicity. It left a lump in my throat, and I cannot think of it even today without emotion. That was religion at its finest."[2]

Long years after that experience, he said that his father's habit of reading the Bible aloud to him, his brothers and his sisters, and that gentle preacher's attitude when only one worshiper showed up at church—and he was only a boy—were two of the strong

64

influences that encouraged him to make some of the greatest motion pictures that were ever filmed.

The boy was Cecil B. DeMille and he became a world-renowned motion picture producer. He directed such pictures as *The Ten Commandments, The King of Kings,* and *The Sign of the Cross.*

There is no way to tell what great wheels we may set in motion when we encourage a child. Remember: Abraham Lincoln was once a boy; Florence Nightingale was once a little girl; and Billy Graham was once a lad.

How can we bless a child and, in turn, help that child to be a blessing to others? Jesus shows us how.

We Must Encourage the Child

The mothers wanted their children blessed by the popular Teacher, but the disciples didn't want the Master to be bothered. When the mothers brought their children to Jesus to be blessed, Mark said the Lord's "disciples rebuked those that brought them" (v. 13). All the mothers wanted was encouragement for their little ones. All they got from the disciples was discouragement. But verse 16 shows how Jesus encouraged the children: "And he took them up in his arms, put his hands upon them, and blessed them."

When Robert Burns was at the height of his popularity in Scotland, he visited a home one day in which there was a teenage boy. Seeing a picture hanging on the wall and wanting to draw the boy out, Burns asked the lad to explain the painting. Burns wanted to know all about it: who painted it, where it was painted, and any other detail the boy could recall.

The lad, so encouraged that the most famous figure in Scotland had asked him to do something for him, went into great detail explaining the meaning of the painting.

On another occasion—whether true or apocryphal I cannot say —it is related that Burns told the boy he would be a great person in Scotland someday. "You may even become a great writer," Burns said, in encouraging the boy.

I think of that story each time I read some of the things that boy wrote when he grew to manhood. Among them are *The Lady of the Lake, The Lay of the Last Minstrel,* and *Ivanhoe,* to mention a few. His name was Sir Walter Scott, the greatest romantic novelist in Scotland's history. I have often wondered how much the encouragement of Robert Burns contributed to the making of Sir Walter Scott.

Secondly, to bless a child:

We Must Set a Good Example Before the Child
The example the disciples set was terrible. Frustrated, tired, anxious about their Master's comfort, they rebuked the tender-hearted mothers for bringing their little ones to the Lord.

But Jesus would have none of their impatience with the children. Mark said that when Jesus saw how the disciples were treating the children "he was much displeased" (v. 14). He then added in verse 15: "Whosoever shall not receive the kingdom of God as a little child, he shall not enter therein."

Some of the best pottery and china one can buy carries the name Wedgewood. The British company was founded by Josiah Wedgewood who died in 1795.

"The Wedgewood pottery plants were always fascinating to visitors. On one occasion a wealthy young nobleman was one of the interested visitors. As his guide through the plants, he was assigned a likeable lad of about fifteen. As the tour progressed, the nobleman was liberal with his smart wisecracks, interspersed with oaths and bad language. His guide was rather shocked, because Mr. Wedgewood, who was a noble Christian gentleman, had taken a great deal of interest and pride in this particular employee, and had taught him not to use such language and not to make light of the sacred things of life. Following the lad and the nobleman with another group of visitors, Mr. Wedgewood was shocked at the things which he heard.

"After completing his visit through the plants, and seeing the pottery at its different stages, the young nobleman was returned to the office in which he planned to select several choice pieces. Pointing to one which he admired, he asked the owner something about it. Mr. Wedgewood removed it from the shelf and began to describe its beauty as only the creator of a work of art could describe it. As the nobleman put forth his hand to take it from his host, it was dropped to the floor and broke into a hundred pieces.

"Angered at the apparent carelessness of his host, he expressed his feelings rather strongly because he had so much wanted that particular piece of pottery. With the patience and consideration of a father, Mr. Wedgewood leaned forward and said in substance: 'My young friend, I can replace this piece of pottery, I can make another one just as beautiful, but there are things in life which can never be replaced, sacred and holy things which can never be restored. You have destroyed something in the life of the lad who was your guide by the language you used. You have shattered ideals which I have been trying to build into his life these past few years.' "[3]

Emphasizing the importance of being a good example, R. L. Sharpe wrote:

> Isn't it strange that princes and kings,
> And clowns that caper in sawdust rings,
> And common folks like you and me
> Are builders of eternity?
>
> To each is given a bag of tools,
> A shapeless mass and a book of rules;
> And each must make, ere life is flown,
> A stumbling-block or a stepping-stone.[4]

Thirdly, to bless a child:

We Must See the Potential in the Child

When the disciples saw the children, they saw problems. But when Jesus saw the children, He saw potential. Their potential is so great, Jesus said as he scolded His thoughtless disciples, that no one gets to heaven unless he has the spirit of a child. The childlike spirit has heavenly potential. That's the greatest potential imaginable.

During the last years of the eighteenth century, a compassionate Scottish Sunday School teacher had a class of poor, needy boys. One of the teacher's friends, a wealthy businessman, said he would give a new suit of clothes to each of the teacher's boys.

The suits were given to the boys and the most unpromising one of the lot, named Bob, came to Sunday School only a time or two after he received his new suit. When his teacher found him the suit was torn and dirty, so the prosperous businessman gave Bob a second suit. But, after a Sunday or two, Bob disappeared again.

The teacher was ready to give up, but the businessman insisted that he give Bob a third suit provided he would promise to attend regularly. Bob promised he would come, accepted the suit, and was eventually won to Jesus.

The poor boy was Robert Morrison, who became a pioneer missionary to China. He was sent to China in 1807 by the London Missionary Society. When the East India Company refused Morrison passage to China, as it had refused passage to India for William Carey, Morrison sailed to Canton on an American ship. But when he arrived in China, he was neither welcomed by the Chinese, the East India Company, nor the Jesuit missionaries at Macao. Discouragement met him at every turn.

On his way to China, a skeptical shipowner in New York asked the young missionary: " 'So then, Mr. Morrison, you really expect to make an impression on the idolatry of the great Chinese Empire? . . . Quickly and with emphasis came the reply, 'No, sir, but I expect God will.' "[5]

Morrison's contribution to the work of Christ in China was monumental. In 1813 he translated the New Testament into Chinese. In 1818 he finished the translation of the entire Bible. In addition, he published a score of different works, "including a Chinese grammar and his monumental dictionary of six volumes and 4,500 pages. In 1814, after seven long years of patient toil, he baptized in Macao, Tsai A-ko, the first-known Chinese Christian convert. In 1824 Morrison visited England and was received with honor by the churches and also by the King. He returned to China in 1826 and died there in 1834."[6]

Morrison's missionary service in China covered twenty-seven years and yet he baptized fewer than a dozen converts. But by giving the Scriptures to the Chinese people in their own language, he made a contribution that shall last forever. " 'By the Chinese Bible,' he said himself, 'when dead, I shall yet speak.' "[7]

If we are going to be a blessing to the children, we must see their potential, as did Jesus.

Finally, to bless a child:

We Must Lead the Child to Jesus

"And they brought young children to him, that he should touch them" (Mark 10:13). "They" could refer to fathers, mothers, or friends. They were bringing the children to Jesus in order to have them blessed by the Teacher. They wanted the very best for their children.

When I was in the seminary, one of our professors told us one day that he and his wife prayed for their children when they were small that they would never know a full day of active rebellion against God. "We prayed," he said, "that when they first discovered they were sinners, they would trust Jesus as their personal Savior." That, of course, is the ideal.

The late Dr. R. G. Lee gave some startling statistics about the importance of leading a child to Jesus. Lee wrote: "Nineteen out of every twenty who become Christians do so before they reach the age of twenty-five. After twenty-five, only one in 10,000; after thirty-five, only one in 50,000; after forty-five, only one in 200,000; after fifty-five, only one in 300,000; after sixty-five, only one in 500,000; (and) after seventy-five, only one in 700,000."[8]

In a large class in the seminary I attended, the professor asked those who had been saved before they were ten or twelve to raise their hand. And a huge majority responded.

In his commentary on Acts, Alexander Maclaren, the great English preacher, writes about people who would give everything they have if they could blot out the memories of sins committed before they trusted Jesus as their Savior. Those who do not trust Christ early, he says, will fight habits and memories that will hurt them all of their days. Although Jesus will forgive our sins, Maclaren warns, those memories will sting and burn for life.

"It is a better thing not to know the depths of evil than to know them and to have been raised from them. You will escape infinite sorrows by an early cleaving to Christ your Lord," he encouraged.

Maclaren's wisdom is well-taken. The best thing one can do for a child is to lead him/her to a conscious, strong commitment to Jesus Christ in his/her early years.

And who is the person who most influences a child toward an early acceptance of Jesus Christ? According to John W. Drakeford in his book, *Psychology in Search of a Soul*, a survey taken at

Southwestern Baptist Theological Seminary, Fort Worth, Texas, revealed that in 64 percent of the cases the mother was the most influential; in 48 percent, a minister; in 44 percent, the father; and in 28 percent, a Sunday School teacher.

A certain preacher, so the story goes, returned from a revival meeting and reported to his deacons that there had been thirteen and one-half conversions in the meeting.

"That's marvelous," said one of his more pious deacons. "What a wonderful thing is that there were thirteen adults saved and one child."

"No," the pastor replied, "you misunderstand. There were thirteen children and one man past fifty who were saved."

When we win the children to Jesus, both a soul and a life are saved. And that's Christ's ideal.

Benjamin P. Browne told about the bombarding of Vienna, Austria, by Napoleon in 1805. During the bombardment, a school building was hit, blowing out the walls and windows. Inside the building was an eight-year-old boy named Franz who was practicing on the piano. When the shell hit the school building, young Franz fell to the floor and hid his face in his arms in terror. Then through the dust and debris, he heard the calm voice of his schoolmaster calling out, "Franz! Franz! Are you all right?" The boy was Franz Schubert, the great Austrian composer.

The schoolmaster's question is a valid one. We ought to be concerned not only about the physical welfare of the children, but especially concerned about their spiritual welfare. But, alas, rather than being sensitive to the children as the gentle Savior was, the unconcerned attitude of the disciples toward the children may better characterize us.

Conclusion

At Baylor University in Waco, Texas, the memory of Dr. J. B. Tidwell lingers as a blessed benediction. For many years Tidwell was head of the Baptist school's Bible department.

Tidwell's father, Francis, was an early-day pioneer preacher. One April day in 1879, the elder Tidwell left home for his preaching appointment for the day. Ann Tidwell, his wife and the mother of his children, was left in bed with a severe headache.

Suddenly, from the dimly lighted bedroom came an urgent cry

from Mrs. Tidwell. Young J. B. hurried inside and his mother told him that she was terribly sick and urged him to hurry down to his uncle's house to get help.

Tidwell then adds this sad comment: " 'I went back to the house after calling my aunt. My little brother and sister were on the bed with mother. She put her hand on my head and told me that she thought she was going to die. She said that she was going to heaven to live with God, and wanted me to come to her sometime. She prayed for me to be kept by God and finally to have a home with her in the Divine Father's house. In a little while she was unconscious and never knew her boy any more. My heart was tender and melted then. I remembered the little prayers mother had taught us. I wish somebody had been there to lead me to Christ.' "[9]

One wonders how much the influence and prayers of Tidwell's godly mother contributed to his character and ministry. Few men in modern Christian history have meant as much to the kingdom of God as did J. B. Tidwell. One would probably not be too far wrong to hazard a guess that the prayers and blessings of his mother contributed more than any other factor to his making.

Notes

1. Lewis L. Dunnington, *Power to Become* (New York: The Macmillan Company, 1956), p. 91.

2. Ibid.

3. Cited in R. L. Middleton, *The Accents of Life* (Nashville: Broadman Press, 1948), pp. 103-104.

4. Ibid., pp. 102-103.

5. Robert H. Glover, *The Progress of World-Wide Missions* (New York, London: Harper and Brothers Publishing Company, 1953), p. 135.

6. Ibid, p. 136.

7. Ibid.

8. R. G. Lee, *Modern Illustrations for Public Speakers* (Grand Rapids: Zondervan Publishing House, 1955), p. 92.

9. Robert A. Baker, *J. B. Tidwell Plus God* (Nashville: Broadman Press, 1946), p. 9.

The Book of God

Scripture: 2 Timothy 3:14 to 4:4

Introduction

What is the Bible?

According to the Russian *Dictionary of Foreign Words,* the Bible is "A collection of different legends, mutually contradictory and written at different times, and full of historical errors, issued by the churches as a 'holy book.' "[1]

But Christians believe the Bible is a holy, perfect book given to us by God. Paul said these are "the holy Scriptures" and that they are "given by inspiration of God" (vv. 15-16).

About the Bible, Abraham Lincoln said: "I believe the Bible is the best gift God has ever given to man." George Washington said: "It is impossible to rightly govern the world without God and the Bible." Patrick Henry said: "The Bible is worth all of the books which have ever been printed."

About the Bible, Andrew Jackson said: "That book, sir, is the rock on which our Republic rests."

Robert E. Lee said: "In all my perplexities and distresses, the Bible has never failed to give me light and strength."

Daniel Webster said: "If we abide by the principles taught in the Bible, our country will go on prospering and to prosper."

Look at what Paul said about the Book of God.

It Is a Perfect Book

"Thou has known the holy scriptures" (v. 15). The late Dr. Robert G. Lee used to say that the Bible does not contain one error to lead one soul one foot astray.

It is from God.—Only that which is from God is "holy" (v. 15). All that is "given by the inspiration of God" is holy (v. 16). Harold Fickett wrote in *Baptist Beliefs* that the Bible claims divine inspi-

72

ration for itself 3,125 times—2,600 times in the Old Testament;
525 times in the New Testament.

It is about Jesus—He is its subject: "Which is in Christ Jesus" (v.
15). Anything that is about Jesus is perfect for He is perfect. Re-
former Martin Luther said, "The Bible is the cradle in which
Christ lives." In his book *Living All Your Life*, John A. Redhead
tells about a Scottish minister who was once asked to suggest a
good book on the life of Jesus. In reply, the minister answered,
"Have you tried the one by Dr. Luke?"

Redhead adds: "The Bible is the inspired record of the revela-
tion and of the character and purpose of God, culminating in Jesus
Christ, for the salvation of men and the establishment of His kingdom. The center of the Bible is Christ. It was said of Dwight L.
Moody's preaching that no matter where his sermon started from
in the Bible, he lost no time in hot-footing it to Christ."[2]

It Is a Powerful Book

"Thou hast known the holy scriptures, which are able to make
the wise unto salvation" (v. 15). "Able" is a Greek word that means
strength, ability, power (Thayer). The power of the Bible is illustrated by the story of the survivors of the *Bounty* and Pitcairn
Island.

In 1790, nine sailors from the British ship *Bounty*, along with six
men and twelve women from Tahiti landed on Pitcairn Island.
After one of the sailors learned to distill alcohol, all on the island
became debauched and drunken. Finally, only one British sailor
was left alive, along with several of the native women and several
half-breed children. The sailor found a Bible and began to teach
the Scriptures and the colony was transformed. When the USS
Topaz stopped at Pitcairn in 1808, they found a thriving community—no liquor, no jail, no crime. The power of the Word of God had
changed the island.

It is powerful in showing us our need.—"Which are able to
make thee wise" (v. 15). This wisdom from above shows us our
need of the Savior.

It is powerful in leading us to grace.—"Unto salvation through
faith which is in Christ Jesus" (v. 15). Charles Spurgeon, the great
English pastor, visited Albert Hall where he was to preach the

following Sunday. Testing the acoustics, he quoted 1 John 1:7: "The blood of Jesus Christ his Son cleanseth us from all sin." He learned later that a painter who was working in the hall heard the voice of Spurgeon quoting from the Scriptures and was saved.

It Is a Profitable Book

"Profitable for doctrine, for reproof, for correction, for instruction in rightousness: That the man of God may be perfect, thoroughly furnished unto all good works" (vv. 16-17).

It is said that Alexander the Great's most-prized possession was a copy of Homer's *Illiad*. Given to him by Aristotle, his teacher, the *Illiad* tells about the Trojan Wars which were fought nearly one thousand years before Alexander's time. Homer's book was kept under Alexander's pillow, by the side of his dagger. The precious thing was kept close at hand. For Alexander, the *Illiad* was a profitable book.

It is profitable because of the instruction it gives.—"All scripture is given by inspiration of God, and is profitable for doctrine" (v. 16). It not only tells us how to be saved, but how to live after we are saved.

In their book *Twenty Centuries of Great Preaching*, Fant and Pinson relate that the grandmother of Methodist Evangelist Sam Jones (1847-1906) read the Bible through thirty-seven times on her knees. Jones' mother died when he was only a child but this godly grandmother's life and love for the Word of God were great influences for good on Jones. The Bible's instruction, learned from his godly grandmother, served Jones well all his days.

It is profitable because of the correction it gives.—"Profitable . . . for reproof, for correction, for instruction in rightousness" (v. 16).

Oliver Cromwell, England's ruler for a time in the seventeenth century, had a rather large wart on his face. When he went to have his portrait painted he told the artist, "Paint me just as I am, wart and all." The Bible paints us "warts and all," showing us what we are and then showing us what we ought to be.

It Is a Preachable Book

The late R. C. Campbell wrote: "Its theme is the greatest, its message the sweetest, its purpose the noblest, its scope the broadest, its motive the highest, its stream of influence the deepest, its light the brightest, its ideal the most heavenly, and its voice the most vibrant in all the world!"[3] We need Bible preaching, not just preaching about the Bible (see 4:1-4).

The charge to preach it.—"I charge thee . . . Preach the word" (vv. 1-2). Paul's final charge to the young pastor, Timothy, was "preach the word." *Charge,* according to Wuest, "was used to call the gods and men to witness." Timothy is called to bear witness through preaching. *Preach,* Wuest said, calls "to his mind the Imperial Herald, spokesman of the emperor, proclaiming in a formal, grave, and authoritative manner which must be listened to, the message which the Emperor gave him to announce." *Word* is the whole body of revealed scriptural truth.

About the divine call to preach, William Barclay wrote in *A Spiritual Autobiography:* "Let preaching become a work to be avoided except by those who believe they must do it. Constraint has been a mark of preaching since Moses became aware of his stammering tongue and Jeremiah felt the fire in his bones. As Paul said long ago: 'Necessity is laid upon me. Woe to me if I do not preach the gospel!' (1 Cor. 9:16)."[4]

The reason to preach it (see 4:3-4).—Henry Wadsworth Longfellow went to church one Sunday morning and when he got home he wrote in his diary: "John Ware of Cambridge preached a good sermon. I applied it to myself." The reason for preaching is that people need it. They need true preaching because of false doctrines and false prophets (vv. 3-4).

Zig Ziglar, in his *Confessions of a Happy Christian,* relates that in the Louvre there are three and one-half miles of books on science which are outdated. Carefully thought out scientific facts, dependable and irrefutable in their day, are now worthless, he says. But the Word of God, which we are charged to preach, is as fresh as this morning's newspaper and speaks to every problem faced by mankind. Its relevancy is sufficient reason to preach it.

Conclusion

A. Z. Conrad gives a marvelous tribute to the Book of God when he wrote:

> Century follows century — There it stands.
> Empires rise and fall and are forgotten — There it stands.
> Dynasty succeeds dynasty — There it stands.
> Kings are crowned and uncrowned — There it stands.
> Emperors decree its extermination — There it stands.
> Atheists rail against it — There it stands.
> Agnostics smile cynically — There it stands.
> Profane prayerless punsters caricature it — There it stands.
> Unbelief abandons it — There it stands.
> Higher critics deny its claim to inspiration — There it stands.
> The flames are kindled about it — There it stands.
> The tooth of time gnaws but makes no dent in it — There it stands.
> Infidels predict its abandonment — There it stands.
> Modernism tries to explain it away — There it stands.[5]

Notes

1. Margaret Applegarth, *Men as Trees Walking* New York: Harper and Row Publishers, 1952), p. 136.

2. John A. Redhead, *Living All Your Life* (New York/Nashville: Abingdon Press, 1961), p. 130.

3. R. C. Campbell, *Keeping the Foundation* (Nashville: Broadman Press, 1946), p. 16.

4. William Barclay, *A Spiritual Autobiography* (Grand Rapids: William B. Eerdmans Publishing Co. 1975), p. 76.

5. Walter B. Knight, *Knight's Master Book of New Illustrations* (Grand Rapids: William B. Eerdmans Publishing Co., 1956), p. 26.

Everybody's Favorite Verse

Scripture: John 3:16-18

Introduction

Years ago when I was a young pastor, a man in our community accidentally shot his little six-year-old boy. The man's wife was a Christian, and the family attended church together, but the husband and father was not a Christian.

He and a friend were doing some target practicing with a .22 caliber rifle when the little boy came home from school. Not knowing his father was shooting the rifle in the backyard, the little boy ran around to the backyard and stepped in front of the gun just as his father pulled the trigger. The slug tore through the boy's head, knocking him out of a pair of cowboy boots.

A few days after I had held the boy's funeral, I got down on my knees in my study and asked the Lord to help me lead the father to know the Savior. As I prayed, there grew in my heart the irresistible conviction that I ought to drive out to his farm and talk to him about his need for a Savior. Not knowing whether he was home, I drove the ten miles out to his farm home, knocked on the door, and he answered.

"Bobby," I said, "I have come to tell you how to be saved." And Bobby replied: "J. B., I was plowing in the field until a few minutes ago and I became so convicted of my need for Christ that I came home and told my wife that I had never in all my life felt so lost."

I told Bobby how to be saved and immediately he made his commitment to Jesus. The following Sunday morning he made public his profession of faith in Christ, and a few days later I baptized him in obedience to Christ's command. And, in the days to come, I saw a mighty transformation take place in his life.

The most important thing in the world is to be a Christian.

Nothing—health, possessions, family—is more important than trusting in Christ as one's personal Savior.

The best-known verse in the Bible addresses our greatest need. It is John 3:16 and it's everybody's favorite verse.

What God Has Done to Save Us

He loves us.—"For God so loved the world" (v. 16*a*). He loves the "world" but He also loves "whosoever." It is a personal love.

In his book *My Cup Runneth Over,* R. L. Middleton told about an Englishman who had a beautiful estate on the Yorkshire coast from which he could look in all directions. One day as he and his daughter were admiring the beautiful landscape, he told her to look up and she would see the beautiful sky; to look down and she would see the blue sea; to look out and she would see the white-capped sea stretching toward the horizon; and to look around and she would see their beautiful home. "Just so high, deep, wide, and broad is the love of God," he said to her. And the little girl replied, "Why Daddy, we're standing right in the middle of God's love aren't we?" John told us that we are living in the middle of God's love: "For God so loved the world" (v. 16*a*).

He gave his Son to save us.—"That he gave his only begotten Son" (v. 16*b*).

John Bunyan, the author of *The Pilgrim's Progress,* was drafted to serve as a soldier during England's civil war, to fight in the battle of Leicester. But a young man volunteered to serve in Bunyan's place, as the custom of that day permitted. The young man was killed in battle, and Bunyan later said: "He took my place; and, coming to the seige, as he stood sentinel he was shot in the head by a musket bullet, and died." The soldier gave his life to save Bunyan.

Stenberg, an eighteenth century German artist, was saved as he worked on a painting of the crucifixion of Jesus. When he started the painting, he was not a Christian. But as he painted the portrait of a gypsy girl, she saw the painting of the crucifixion and asked Stenberg, "Did he die for you?" This started Stenberg to thinking. As he finished the crucifixion, he was saved. Later, Nicholas Zinzendorf, the founder of the Moravian Church, was saved as he viewed Stenberg's painting. It was hanging in the gallery at Dusseldorf, Germany, and Zinzendorf stopped to look at it one day. Zinzendorf was saved as he read the words written beneath the painting; "This I did for thee; what hast thou done for me?"

What We Must Do to Be Saved

In his book *From Cana to Calvary*, Harry Rimmer told about a sailing vessel which was driven far off course by a storm. After the storm subsided, the sailors discovered their water supply had been contaminated by sea water. On the second day without water, the crew, not knowing what they would do, saw another sailing vessel approaching them. "We need fresh water. Can you help us?" they called out. And much to their surprise, the vessel's captain laughed loudly and told them to let down their buckets because they had sailed into a channel of fresh water. Salvation is available to each of us, but we must take it. Two things are involved.

We must repent of our sins.—Sin is the possession of a nature that has as its chief characteristic rebellion against God. Repentance is turning from that attitude (Matt. 3:2; 4:17; Mark 1:15; 6:12.) A. H. Strong defines repentance: "Repentance is that voluntary change in the mind of the sinner in which he turns from sin." A man traveling by foot one day asked a boy how far it was to a certain place. The boy answered that the way the man was going it was 25,000 miles. "But," the boy said, "if you will turn around and go in the opposite direction it will be about two miles." Repentance is a spiritual "turning around."

We must trust in Jesus Christ.—"Whosoever believeth in him" (v. 16c); "He that believeth on him" (v. 18). It is not just believing about Jesus but believing in Him—trusting Him as one's Savior.

Charles Haddon Spurgeon was saved one snowy Sunday morning in a church at Colchester, England, as the visiting Primitive Methodist minister quoted Isaiah 45:22: "Look unto me, and be ye saved, all the ends of the earth: for I am God, and there is none else." A deeply convicted sixteen-year-old lad, Spurgeon thought he was beyond grace. He wanted to be saved and had prayed to be saved, but he didn't know the way. In later life Spurgeon wrote: "What could I do? . . . I knew it was said, 'Believe on the Lord Jesus Christ and thou shalt be saved,' but I did not know what it was to believe in Christ." On that Sunday morning in a little Primitive

Methodist chapel, with no more than fifteen people present, an unlearned preacher quoted that passage to Spurgeon as though he were the only one present. As he heard the minister say, "Look unto Me . . . Look unto Me; I am hanging on the cross. Look! I am dead and buried. Look unto Me; I will rise again. Look unto Me; I ascend; I am sitting at the Father's right hand. O! look to Me! look to Me!"[1] That morning Spurgeon trusted in Jesus and was saved.

What We Are Saved From

He saves us from a wasted life.—Physician A. Dudley Dennison Jr., in his book *Windows, Ladders, and Bridges,* tells about the conversion of Jim Vaus. As a young man, Vaus was expelled both from college and a Bible institute for stealing. As an army captain during World War II, he was convicted of stealing federal property. Out of the army, he free-lanced as a wiretapper in Los Angeles. He next worked on a delaying electronic device for crime syndicate head Micky Cohen that would enable gamblers in distant cities to place winning bets on horses before the results of the race were announced. Then Jim Vaus attended a Billy Graham Crusade and was saved. To repay large debts he owed, Vaus sold his car, house, and everything of value. And for many years after his conversion, he ministered to gang leaders in the East Harlem area of New York City. Christ saved Jim Vaus from a ruined life.

He saves us from hell.—"Whosoever believeth in him should not perish" (v. 16*c*); "He that believeth on him is not condemned: but he that believeth not is condemned already, because he hath not believed in the name of the only begotten Son of God" (v. 18). A. T. Robertson says *perish* means "to destroy." Contrast "perish," "saved," and "eternal life." Robertson says about "condemned": "Is not judged. . . . Trust in Christ prevents condemnation, for he takes our place and pays the penalty for sin for all who put their case in his hands (Rom. 8:32 *f.*). The believer in Christ as Saviour does not come into judgment (John 5:24). . . . Judgment has already been passed on the one who refuses to believe in Christ as the Saviour sent by the Father, the man who is not willing to come to Christ for life (5:40)."[2]

In describing the eternal hopelessness of the unsaved, the late R. C. Campbell wrote: "An inscription over the huge, hideous iron gates of the prison de la Roquette, Paris, which is set apart for criminals who are condemned to death, reads, 'Abandon hope, all ye who enter here!' This inscription sends a chill of horror through those who read it."[3] But a million times worse, and far more than that, is the hopelessness of those who live and die without Jesus, the only one who can save us from hell.

What God Gives Us When He Saves Us

"Whosoever believeth in him should not perish, but have everlasting life" (v. 16*d*).

Eternal life is our present possession.—It is both quality of life and duration of life. The believer already has a quality of life like Jesus has: "We are in him that is true, even in his Son Jesus Christ. This is the true God, and eternal life" (1 John 5:20*d*): "And I give unto them eternal life; and they shall never perish, neither shall any man pluck them out of my hand" (John 10:28).

Eternal life is our future possession.—John 14:3: "And if I go and prepare a place for you, I will come again, and receive you unto myself; that where I am, there ye may be also." It is heavenly, eternal life.

Conclusion

It was my privilege, years ago, to have Commander Mitsuo Fuchida speak in the church where I was pastor. Before the service, Fuchida and I had dinner together and he told me about his conversion.

He was flying the lead plane and was the first one to drop his bombs when the Japanese attacked Pearl Harbor on December 7, 1941. With 182 planes following him, he picked a battleship anchored at Pearl Harbor, let out a scream of exultation, and released his bombs.

In a nearby power plant at Pearl Harbor, engineer R. E. Peterson heard the explosion of the bombs and pulled a lever sounding the first alarm to the sleeping naval base.

On January 5, 1958, another Sunday, the two men met. Both Peterson and Fuchida had become Christians—Peterson was a Baptist and Fuchida was a Presbyterian minister. On that morning Fuchida preached in Hawaii's Wainae Baptist Church where Peterson was a member.

Former enemies, the two men shared a common bond: each had been saved through the blood of Jesus.

Notes
1. R. L. Middleton, *Don't Disappoint God* (Nashville: Broadman Press, 1951), pp. 19-20.
2. A. T. Robertson, *Word Pictures in the New Testament, Volume V* (Nashville: Broadman Press, 1932), pp. 51-52.
3. R. C. Campbell, *The Christ of the Centuries* (Nashville: Broadman Press, 1947), p. 152.

Work: God's Gift

Scripture: John 9:4

Introduction

William Hickling Prescott was a great American historian. Born in Salem, Massachusetts, in 1796, Prescott was a Harvard man.

During the time Prescott was a student at Harvard, a fellow student threw a piece of hard bread striking Prescott in the eye. He lost the use of the eye and, in time, the other eye, burdened by its increased work, began to fail. Soon Prescott was all but sightless.

A dedicated historian, Prescott didn't let his handicap stop him. Writing with the special aid of an instrument that kept lines straight, he continued to write.

In 1838 he published *The History of the Reign of Ferdinand and Isabella the Catholic.* In 1843 and 1847, he published two of his greatest works: *The History of the Conquest of Mexico* and *The History of the Conquest of Peru.*

For years, because of his poor eyesight, he could only write an hour a day. And sometimes those hours were broken down into ten-minute periods. But he courageously plodded on.

When he died at Salem in 1859, he left behind sixteen volumes which deal chiefly with Spain, the Americas, and the Protestant Reformation. He was truly one of history's outstanding historians.

What would Prescott have been without his work? Perhaps he would have frittered away his talents in purposeless living. But Prescott's work made him. It was his life. Work was God's gift to him.

But work is God's gift to each of us. Virginia Ely said that "Every man who is born into this world represents a fresh thought of God and has a work that is born within him."[1]

Quoting American evangelist Dwight L. Moody, Ely said that

the first words that Christ ever spoke on earth had to do with His work: " 'Wist ye not that I must be about my Father's business?' " And she adds, "You will find that during his ministry, he toiled early and late in the work."[2]

In John 9:4 Jesus talked about His work: "I must work the works of him that sent me, while it is day: the night cometh, when no man can work."

On this Sunday before Labor Day, let us think about work, God's special gift to each of us.

God Gives Us Work to Do

Each of us has his work. One of Thomas Carlyle's beatitudes was, "Blessed is he who has found his work."

It is personal work.—Jesus said, "*I* must work. . . ." He had His work. We have our work. God has given work to each of us.

Robert Henri (1865-1929) was an American portrait and landscape painter. He specialized in the portraits of children.

On one occasion, Henri went to a New York art gallery for a private showing of paintings. As he was admiring a portrait by John Singer Sargent (1856-1925), a well-known artist of that era, Henri heard the man standing next to him say, "At last they have given me a place."

Not wanting to ignore the proud statement of the stranger, Henri asked the man which of the paintings was his.

Pointing proudly at the painting hanging before him, the stranger replied, "That one."

"But John Sargent painted that one," Henri replied.

"Yes," the stranger answered, "I think Sargent did paint the picture. But I made the frame."

God gives us our work, and He personalizes it. He fits it to our talent.

It is important work.—In his book *The Accents of Life,* R. L. Middleton related a story told by A. Lindsay Glegg about the coronation of King George V of England.

When the king was crowned in 1910, a businessman sat at his window above the street to watch the magnificent parade that attended the coronation. However, he was distracted by a fifteen-year-old boy who, hoping to get a good view of the parade, was hanging precariously from a lamppost.

Seeing how uncomfortable the boy seemed to be, the business-man went down to the street and pushed his way through the crowd until he stood beneath the lamppost.

When he asked the boy how long he had been perched on the crossbar of the lamppost, he replied he had been there since 3:30 that morning. Inviting the boy to come down, the businessman took the lad upstairs where they both comfortably viewed the procession from the man's office window.

As the king's carriage approached, the boy exclaimed: "Look at the lamps on the royal coach. Look how bright and shining they are." As far as he could see the king's coach, the excited boy kept asking, "Did you see how brightly the lamps shone?"

His new friend was confused. Nothing in the procession seemed to impress the boy but the brightly shining lamps on the coach. When the man inquired why the boy was so impressed by the carriage lamps, he replied that he worked at a factory that had been appointed to redecorate the royal coach and that his job had been to polish the lamps.

If your work is honorable work, and I assume it is, then regard-less of what it is, it is important work.

It is delegated work.—Jesus said, "I must work the works of him that sent me." The work of the Heavenly Father had been dele-gated to the Son. And whatever humble or great work God has to do in the world, He is going to delegate it to folks like you and me.

To Michelangelo, God delegated the work of painting and sculpting. God can paint a sunset, but He needed Michelangelo to paint the Sistine Chapel. God can sculpt a Grand Canyon, but He needed Michelangelo to sculpt Moses and David.

As Michelangelo sculpted Moses from an ugly block of marble, the ugly stone came alive for him. It was not just marble. To him it was flesh, bone, and blood. When he was finished, Michelangelo picked up his chisel, struck Moses on the knee, and shouted: "Speak Moses! Speak!" And on the knee of Moses one can clearly see the indentation made by Michelangelo's chisel.

God Gives Us Time to Do Our Work

Horace Greeley was one of America's most influential newspaper editors. Founder and editor of the *New York Tribune*, Greeley was much involved in the antislavery movement which preceded the Civil War. Perhaps he is best known for his advice, "Go west, young man."

In his book *Wake Up, Make Up and Go*, W. E. Thorn wrote about Greeley: "He did not allow any ordinary disturbance, disappointment or noise to irritate him. He would sit upon the curb of the street, use the top of his tall hat for a desk, and write an editorial for the *New York Tribune* while a great procession went by with bands playing loudly and the street lined with shouting people."[3]

Greeley's careful use of time, no doubt, was one of the reasons for his success. Any person who hopes to live meaningfully, must wisely use the time God has given him or her to do his work.

Horace Mann, an American educator and congressman born in 1796, wrote: "Lost, yesterday, somewhere between sunrise and sunset, two golden hours, each set with sixty diamond minutes. No reward is offered, for they are gone forever."

It must be done at the present time.—Jesus said, "I must work . . . while it is day." Whatever work we have to do, it must be done now for tomorrow never comes.

In one of the old Greek cities there stood long ago a statue. The following conversation between a traveler and the statue was chiseled on the statue's base.

"What is thy name, O statue?"
"I am called Opportunity."
"Who made thee?"
"Lysippus."
"Why art thou on thy toes?"
"To show how quickly I pass by."
"But why is thy hair so long on thy forehead?"
"That men may seize me when they meet me."
"Why, then, is thy head so bald behind?"
"To show that when I have once passed, I cannot be caught."

Long ago, a wise man said that when they are gone, four things do not come back: the spoken word; the sped arrow; time passed; the neglected opportunity.

"While it is day"—while we have the time we must do the work God has given to us.

It must be done because of passing time.—Jesus said He had to work because "the night cometh, when no man can work." Our work, too, must be done now because time is quickly passing. Our work is limited on the left by the wood of the cradle and on the right by the marble of the tomb.

Thomas Carlyle wrote on the flyleaf of his first book, "Cometh Night." Scottish preacher Robert Murray McCheyne sealed his letters with the words of Jesus, "Cometh Night."

English author Dr. Samuel Johnson inscribed the Lord's words, "Cometh Night," on his watch. And Sir Walter Scott had the Savior's words, "Cometh Night," sculpted on the sundial of his home.

"Tempus fugit!" Time flies!

Franz Schubert was working on his Unfinished Symphony when the end came. Frank Grasso, conductor of the Tampa, Florida, Symphoney Orchestra, suddenly died as he was directing Schubert's Unfinished Symphony. English author Charles Dickens, touched by the angel of death, laid his pen down in the middle of a sentence.

"Tempus fugit!" Since time flies we ought to prize it highly, guard it carefully, enjoy it fully, use it wisely, and give thanks for it continually. Whatever work we have to do, let us do it today because time is passing.

God Gives Us a Way to Do Our Work

Michelangelo was history's greatest sculptor. He often kept a block of marble in his bedroom so he could work on it when he couldn't sleep.

Scottish novelist Sir Walter Scott, wrote the novel *Guy Mannering* in six weeks. Ill with a kidney ailment for two years, Scott kept writing, producing *The Heart of Midlothian, The Bride of Lammermoor,* and *Ivanhoe.* Financially bankrupt in 1826, he determined to pay off his $600,000 debt by writing. And during the next two years, he paid back nearly $200,000. Although he suffered a stroke in 1830, he continued to write, completing two more novels in 1831. The next year he died.

Whatever work God gives us to do, He gives us a way to do it.

It must be done faithfully.—The wise preacher wrote: "Whatsoever thy hand findeth to do, do it with thy might" (Eccl. 9:10). I have read that it can be translated, "Do it with both hands."

Long ago, a saint was approached by one of his followers who found the saint hoeing beans in his garden. "Brother," asked the student, "if you knew this was your last day on earth, what would you do?"

"I would finish hoeing this row of beans," the sage replied.

According to Clarence Macartney, a bugle has been sounded every day for 700 years from the steeple of Saint Mary's Church in Cracow, Poland. "The last note on the bugle is always muted and broken, as if some disaster has befallen the bugler. This 700-year commemoration is in memory of a heroic trumpeter who one night sounded a blast on his trumpet and summoned the people to defend their city against the hordes of invading Tartars. As he was sounding the last blast on his trumpet, an arrow from one of the Tartars struck him and killed him. Hence the muffled note at the end."[4]

Whatever work God has given us to do, it must be done faithfully.

It must be done joyously.—One of the keynote words of the New Testament is *joy*. It is to permeate our work as well as our worship.

The late Methodist minister William L. Stidger in his book *There Are Sermons in Stories*, told about the owner of a small drugstore. He hated his work, so he spent his mornings looking for something better and his afternoons at the ball park.

He soon decided it was foolish to leave a business about which he knew something for one about which he knew nothing. So he decided to make the best of what he had. He would build up his business by giving the best service possible.

When a customer who lived near would call in an order on the telephone, the man would repeat each item being ordered and his assistant would fill the order. With the order filled, the owner would keep the customer on the line while the delivery boy dashed out the front door. When the delivery boy reached the customer's house, who was still on the line with the drugstore owner, she would excuse herself for a minute to answer the door. Coming back to the phone she would express great surprise at the quickness with which the order was delivered.

News got around about the drugstore that filled orders so promptly and soon Charles R. Walgreen, founder of the great Walgreen drugstore empire, had more business than he could handle.

Walgreen said his work was easy—like a game—and he soon found great joy in what he once despised.

Conclusion

"The joy of the Lord is your strength," we are told in Nehemiah 8:10. We must, therefore, let His joy fill us in the quietness of the worship hour as well as in the noise of the work place.

Notes

1. Virginia Ely, *Devotions for Personal and Group Worship* (Old Tappan, New Jersey: Fleming H. Revell Company, 1960), p. 89

2. Ibid.

3. W. E. Thorn, *Wake Up, Make Up and Go* (Newton, Kansas: United Printing, Inc., 1971), p. 177.

4. Clarence E. Macartney, *Macartney's Illustrations* (New York, Nashville: Abingdon-Cokesbury Press, 1945), p. 407.

God's Financial Plan

Scripture: 1 Corinthians 16:1-2

Introduction

An Illinois businessman pinned a piece of paper to a dollar bill one day asking everyone who spent the dollar to make a notation telling for what it was spent. He then wrote on the note, "Please send this back to me in two weeks."

When he got the dollar bill back, here is how it had been spent: five times for salary; five times for tobacco; three times for candy; twice for clothing; three times for meals; once for automobile parts; once for groceries; once for laundry; and once for a tube of toothpaste.

And God was left holding the bag! The dollar had not been spent a single time to help support the work of Him who created and sustains both heaven and earth.

A poignant picture of modern man's attitude toward money was dramatically unearthed in the ancient city of Pompeii. As the archaeologists dug in the ruins of the old city, they turned up the lava-encrusted body of a man who was still firmly gripping a bag of coins in his hand. Perhaps he had heard the rumblings of Vesuvius and, as he beat a hasty exit from his home, he remembered his money, returned to get it, and was caught in the holocaust. He had his money, but his money also had him!

But according to Paul, the Christian's attitude toward the use of his money must be different. Since the believer is a new person in Christ, Paul wrote: "Upon the first day of the week let every one of you lay by him in store, as God hath prospered him, that there be no gatherings when I come" (1 Cor. 16:2).

Tithing is God's financial plan for His church. There is no other way. Church cake sales, raffles, and so forth, are surely embarrassments to the Heavenly Father. He has given to the church His financial plan that, when faithfully followed, will care for all the needs of God's work in the world.

It Is a Good Plan

We cannot improve on perfection, and God's plan is perfect: "Bring ye all the tithes into the storehouse, that there may be meat in mine house" (Mal. 3:10a).

God gave it.—Paul had written the Galatian church about the divine plan. Now he told the Corinthians, "Even so do ye" (1 Cor. 16:1). It is a divine commandment given by the Heavenly Father (see Ps. 24:1; Mal. 3:10; Deut. 8:18; Matt. 23:23; Heb. 7).

It is adequate.—Paul told the Corinthians that if they would be faithful in their giving, there would be no need for "gatherings when I come" (1 Cor. 16:2). If all of God's people would bring all of God's money into God's storehouse on God's day, all of God's needs would be provided.

When I was a young pastor, a church in the community dismissed its pastor because he had taken some money out of the offering plates. Up in arms, and incensed that their pastor was a thief, the church summarily dismissed him—and they should have. But I have been trying in these years since it happened to figure out the difference between the pastor taking twenty dollars out of the offering plate and the members of the church stealing God's tithe each Sunday and using it for themselves (Mal. 3:8)!

It Is a Scriptural Plan

"Tithe" and "tithes" appear thirty-six times in the Bible.

It is Bible centered.—Leviticus 27:30-33; Deuteronomy 14:22-24; 1 Chronicles 29:5-29; and so forth.

It is God's only method.—It has been said that one of the books it takes to operate a church is a pocketbook. If we love Jesus, as we say we do, then our love must not stop at the edge of our pocketbook! The church should obediently follow the only financial plan God has given to meet its needs.

It Is a Fair Plan

Paul told the Corinthians that a believer ought to give "as God hath prospered him" (1 Cor. 16:2).

On a percentage basis.—Tithe means "tenth." Everyone cannot give the same amount, but everyone can give the same percentage.

In his book *Wellsprings of Wisdom*, Ralph L. Woods told about a young man who knelt with his pastor and promised God he would tithe his income. At that time the young man was making only forty dollars a week and he gladly agreed to tithe his four dollars. In time, God so blessed him that his tithe sometimes was as much as five hundred dollars a week. He called on his pastor again complaining that tithing was costing him too much money and confessed that though it was no problem when he was tithing four dollars a week, five hundred dollars a week was just too much to give to the church. "I simply can't afford it," he told his pastor.

The wise pastor then suggested that they kneel and pray again and ask God to reduce his income so that he could once more afford to tithe.

Everyone can participate.—"Let every one of you lay by him in store" (1 Cor. 16:2); "Bring ye all the tithes into the storehouse" (Mal. 3:10). Wealthy Joseph provided a place for Christ to be buried; wealthy Nicodemus helped to provide spices for Jesus' burial; and a poor widow gave her two mites—all can participate, for none is too rich or too poor. Author Henry Van Dyke, in his story, "The Mansions," told about a man who, upon arriving in heaven, asked to see his mansion. But the angel replied: "We make the mansions out of the material people send us from the earth—their good deeds, their spiritual power, and you have not sent us any building material."

It Is a Proven Plan

God's financial plan has been proved by millions through the ages. God honors it.

*Time has proved it.—*In the Bible and out of it are sufficient testimonies to prove in a court of law that God's plan works. Millions of believers have practiced it; thousands of churches have been built because of it; thousands of missionaries have served because of it; countless homes have been blessed through it; hospitals, schools, and so forth, have been built as a result of it. Time has proved the dependability and adequacy of God's financial plan.

God blesses it.—He promised He would: "Prove me now here-
with, saith the Lord of hosts, if I will not open you the windows
of heaven and pour you out a blessing, that there shall not be room
enough to receive it" (Mal. 3:10). One of the basic laws of life is
that God gives to givers. Jesus said: "And with what measure ye
mete, it shall be measured to you again" (Matt. 7:2*b*); "Give, and
it shall be given to you; good measure, pressed down, and shaken
together, and running over, shall men give into your bosom"
(Luke 6:38). No one should tithe just to be blessed. But when we
tithe, God promises to bless us.

Conclusion

Physician Dudley Dennison Jr., told about an experience Dr.
Edwin Saint John Ward had when he was in charge of the American hospital in Beirut. A man came to the hospital one day and told
the doctors that he had swallowed twenty-six gold pounds to keep
from being robbed. When the doctors didn't believe his story, the
man shook his stomach and the physicians could hear the coins
clinking. After surgery, Dr. Ward handed the man his gold and the
greedy gleam returned to his eyes.

But there's a better place to put your money for safekeeping.
Invest it in the work of God.

In Memoriam

Scripture: 1 Corinthians 11:23-34

Introduction

One of the strangest memorials in the world stands in an old battlefield at Saratoga, New York. In a secluded part of the cemetery, there is a stone slab upon which has been sculpted the likeness of a military boot for a man's left leg.

On the back of the strange marker these words are inscribed: "Erected by John Watts de Peyster . . . in memory of the 'most brilliant soldier' of the Continental Army. . . ." Who was this soldier identified only as " 'the most brilliant soldier' of the Continental Army?" He was Benedict Arnold, perhaps the most despised man in American history, who was wounded in the left leg in the unsuccessful charge which he led against Quebec. Also, at Bemis Heights, on the Saratoga battlefield, his horse was shot out from under him and a musket ball fractured his left thigh.

A Revolutionary War hero, Arnold was court-martialed in 1779 because of his misuse of Army property. Compassionate General George Washington only reprimanded Arnold but Arnold was so embittered that he decided to get even by betraying his country. Appointed the commandant of West Point, Arnold agreed to sell out the fort to British Major John Andre. When Andre was captured, papers were discovered on him that told of his and Arnold's scheme, but before George Washington could have Arnold arrested, Arnold went over to the British. He later became a brigadier general in the British Army and died in London in 1801 at the age of sixty years.

It was during the years that Arnold was living in exile in England that John Watts de Peyster had the monument erected on the battlefield where Arnold was wounded. De Peyster did not put Arnold's name on the memorial because Arnold was so despised.

In this message on Communion Sunday, we are considering another memorial that has endured nearly 2,000 years. Neither made from marble nor by the hands of men, it is an eternal memorial to Jesus Christ who paid our sin penalty on the cross.

First, it is a reminder of:

Christ's Love for Us

"For I have received of the Lord that which also I delivered unto you, That the Lord Jesus the same night in which he was betrayed took bread: And when he had given thanks, he brake it, and said, Take, eat: this is my body, which is broken for you: this do in remembrance of me" (vv. 23-24).

The apostle John wrote about this divine love in John 3:16: "For God so loved the world, that he gave his only begotten Son, that whosoever believeth in him should not perish, but have everlasting life."

Jesus said to His disciples in John 15:13: "Greater love hath no man than this, that a man lay down his life for his friends."

The bread symbolizes the bruised body of Christ which was offered for our transgressions: "And as they were eating, Jesus took bread, and blessed it, and brake it, and gave it to the disciples, and said, Take, eat; this is my body" (Matt. 26:26).

The cup symbolizes the shed blood of the Savior by which we are saved: "And he took the cup, and gave thanks, and gave it to them, saying, Drink ye all of it; For this is my blood of the new testament, which is shed for many for the remission of sins" (vv. 27-28).

Benjamin Harris Brewster was a brilliant Philadelphia lawyer who served as the attorney general of the United States under Presidents Garfield and Arthur.

As the United States prepared to celebrate its centennial in 1876, Brewster was chosen to give the patriotic speech at the exercises to be held in Philadelphia's Independence Hall. And although Brewster's face was horribly scarred, it is said he had an unusual grace and dignity and a warm, winsome smile. Because of his attitude, his scars were forgotten by the people who heard him on that occasion.

Samuel J. Randall, once speaker of the United States House of

Representatives, relates that on one occasion Brewster was engaged in a legal trial and the opposing counsel, in a moment of anger, referred to Brewster's horribly scarred features. "A moment of awful silence followed. Then speaking in a very low but distinct voice, Brewster said, 'My brother has referred to my scarred face, to the ravages which appear upon my countenance. I will only say that when I was a boy I was playing with my little brother in the library of our home, when by some chance he fell over into the fireplace. I hurried forward to save him. I did save him. But in doing so I myself fell face forward upon the glowing coals, and a skin that was as fair as that of any child, and eyes that were as perfect as those of childhood were in that instant seared by the hot coals, so that I have borne upon my face ever since the terrible story of that misfortune. But I have always been glad that though I myself suffered, I was able to save my little brother from destruction.' When Brewster ceased to speak and was seated, minutes rather than moments of silence prevailed in the court room."[1]

As Brewster's scars were visible reminders of his love for his brother and the sacrifice Brewster had made to save him, so the Lord's Supper is a visible, living memorial to the Savior's love for sinners.

Secondly, it is a reminder of:

Christ's Presence Within Us

Trying to prepare His disciples for His coming death, Jesus told them: "Verily, verily, I say unto you, Except ye eat the flesh of the Son of man, and drink his blood, ye have no life in you. Whoso eateth my flesh, and drinketh my blood, hath eternal life; and I will raise him up at the last day. For my flesh is meat indeed, and my blood is drink indeed. He that eateth my flesh, and drinketh my blood, dwelleth in me, and I in him" (John 6:53-56).

The Lord's Supper symbolizes both Christ's sacrifice for our sins and the believer's union with Him. But we are saved by repentance and faith, not by partaking of the Lord's Supper. Partaking of the bread and the cup testifies to Christ's presence within His people. The single cup from which Jesus and the disciples drank and the single loaf from which they ate, symbolize both their union with Christ and their oneness with each other.

Patriot Benjamin Franklin was a Deist. He believed in God but only as he revealed himself in nature. Franklin was not a believer in the evangelical sense. The fifteenth child in a family of seventeen children, Franklin was born in Boston, Massachusetts, on January 17, 1706. He died on the night of April 17, 1790, at the age of eighty-four.

It is related that when he lay dying, Franklin asked that either a crucifix or a picture of Jesus on the cross be placed in his bedroom. He said he wanted to look "upon the form of the Silent Sufferer." But as we trust in Christ as our personal Savior, we do more than look upon the form of "the Silent Sufferer"—He lives within us and has given to us eternal life.

Herbert V. Prochnow relates a moving story about General Robert E. Lee. "It was in one of the most aristocratic churches of Richmond, Virginia, soon after the Civil War. The rector had just invited the congregation to come forward to kneel at the altar rail to receive Holy Communion. Suddenly almost a gasp of dismay ran through the pews for, down the aisle, alone, came an elderly Negro, an ex-slave, from his seat in the remote rear. He climbed the chancel steps and knelt, but no one stirred. To break bread, even the bread of Christ, with colored ex-slaves simply was 'not done.' No one moved. Then a whitehaired gentleman, obviously beautifully bred, sensed suddenly what was happening. He rose, walked down the aisle, went up the chancel steps and knelt beside the kneeling Negro. It was General Robert E. Lee."[2]

As Lee was a compassionate friend to the poor, penitent black man, so Jesus is our divine friend who lives within us and shares our life—the good and the bad—with us.

Finally, it is a reminder of:

Christ's Return for Us
Paul told the Corinthians: "For as often as ye eat this bread, and drink this cup, ye do shew the Lord's death till he come" (v. 26).

The second coming of Jesus is one of the most-neglected, abused doctrines of the New Testament. But that Christ is coming again is certain and we are told to be ready (Matt. 24—25).

During the Civil War, Sherman, the Yankee general, was laying waste the South. As he marched across Georgia toward the Atlantic, Confederate General Hood marched to the rear of Sherman to cut off his supplies. General Sherman at once dispatched Lieutenant Corse to Allatoona.

On that clear October day, General Sherman watched Lieutenant Corse and his men as they marched away to battle. Finally, from the Kennesaw Mountains, Sherman's flag officer could make out the message that was being signaled from the embattled soldiers at Allatoona. "Corse is here!" it read.

A young officer who was with Sherman's army related this experience to P. P. Bliss, the famous evangelistic singer, who wrote the hymn, "Hold the Fort."

> Ho, my comrades! See the signal
>   Waving in the sky!
> Reinforcements now appearing,
>   Victory is nigh.
>
> "Hold the fort, for I am coming,"
>   Jesus signals still;
> Wave the answer back to heaven,
>   "By Thy grace we will."

The Lord's Supper is a reminder that Jesus is coming again.

Conclusion

General Robert E. Lee was a fine Christian gentleman. When I go to Richmond, Virginia, the second and final capital of the Confederacy, I walk down Monument Avenue to see the magnificent statue of General Lee astride his horse, Traveller, which stands in the middle of the thoroughfare.

An old Confederate veteran who had served in the terrible war with Lee was standing there admiring the statue one day when a passerby stopped. Moved almost to tears, the old Rebel said, "I have seen it silhouetted against the setting sun, and it was beautiful. I have seen it at noontime with all the glory of the sun radiating from it, and it was beautiful. I have seen it covered with snow in the wintertime, and it was beautiful. I have seen it dozens of times, and each time it was beautiful."

The Lord's Supper is beautiful to the believer because of the blessed one to whom it points. And when we observe it, we do so in remembrance of Him.

Notes

1. G. Hall Todd, *Culture and the Cross* (Grand Rapids: Baker Book House, 1959), p. 24.

2. Herbert V. Prochnow, *Speaker Source Book of Stories, Illustrations, Epigrams and Quotations* (Grand Rapids: Baker Book House, 1955), p. 44.

A Grateful Heart

Scripture: Psalm 150:1-6

Introduction

Ian MacPherson tells about traveling across England by train one hot summer day. As the train rolled to a stop in a little village, through the open windows of the car MacPherson could hear someone outside shouting, "Praise! Praise! Praise!"

MacPherson said he stuck his head out the window almost expecting to see a bearded Hebrew psalmist singing one of the canticles of the Old Testament. He later learned, however, that it was simply the conductor calling out the name of the local station which was P-R-A-Z-E.

MacPherson later told the conductor that it must be a wonderful thing always to "live in praise!"

I don't know the name of the psalmist who wrote Psalm 150, and I don't know the name of the town where he lived, but I know the kind of attitude in which he lived. Thirteen times in these six brief verses this grateful psalmist speaks about praise. Although he is a stranger to me, I know that this good brother who lived long ago had a grateful heart.

Can you think of anything we need to cultivate more than a grateful heart? To live in an attitude of praise would make life sweeter and better for all of us.

This psalm is very appropriate for the Sunday before Thanksgiving Day. Therefore, as we look at it this morning, let me show you four things that relate to a grateful heart.

First, a grateful heart finds:

Someone to Whom to Give Thanks

In *Knight's Master Book of New Illustrations*, Walter B. Knight tells about the sinking of the Scottish trawler, the *Theresa Boyle*, by Nazi bombers in the North Sea during World War II. The ship went down so quickly that the small crew barely escaped with their lives. It was a bitterly cold February day and, because of the cold and exhaustion, one by one the crew members fell back exhausted, unable to help with the rowing. After they had been in the cold water for more than fifty hours, they had all but given up hope of being rescued when they heard droning airplane engines in the near distance. The plane made a low pass over the lifeboat and then headed off fifteen miles away to guide two minesweepers back to the lifeboat. The airplane then circled above the boat until the entire crew had been rescued. Seeing its work was done, it flew away, and had gone about two miles when one of the rescue ships called the plane back. The pilot asked if anything was wrong and the minesweeper signaled that everything was all right and that the survivors simply wanted to say, "Thank you!"

This psalmist reminds us at Thanksgiving time that there is someone to whom we can give thanks every day. In each of these six verses, he pinpoints the one to whom to give thanks: "Praise ye the Lord. Praise God in his sanctuary: praise him in the firmament of his power" (v. 1). Each of verses 2-5 begins with "Praise him," and verse 6 closes with the statement, "Praise ye the Lord."

There is someone behind your good fortune and abundant blessings. But it isn't Lady Luck. And it's neither a rabbit's foot nor a horoscope. The one behind your good fortune is the Heavenly Father. He is the one to whom to give thanks.

Katherine Mansfield, the late British short-story writer, once wrote to a friend: "I have just finished my new book. I finished it last night at ten-thirty and said, 'Thanks be to God!' I wish there were a God. I am longing to praise Him, to thank Him."[1]

Secondly, the grateful heart finds:

Some Place in Which to Give Thanks

Jenny Lind (1820-1887), a Swedish soprano, was one of the most famous singers of the nineteenth century, and her rich and warm voice won for her the title, "The Swedish Nightingale." Once when she was on a visit to Northern Wales, her host took her up to the top of a hill behind his house so she could see the Welsh mountains. It ws a magnificent evening and the setting sun was wrapping everything in gold. Touched by the creative ability of God, Jenny Lind gazed silently at the scene for some minutes and then stepped up on a slab of rock where she began to sing Joseph Haydn's hymn of praise, "The Marvelous Work." She had found a place in which to offer her vocal thanks to almighty God. And her host and friends were so moved they could not speak of it in years to come without great emotion.

Like "The Swedish Nightingale," the psalmist had found his place of thanksgiving: "In his sanctuary . . . in the firmament of his power" (v. 1).

Any place is an appropriate place to give thanks, but there is a special place that has been provided. It is the house of God: "Enter into his gates with thanksgiving, and into his courts with praise: be thankful unto him, and bless his name" (Ps. 100:4).

But also, a grateful heart has:

Something for Which to Give Thanks

The *Mayflower* left Plymouth, England, September 6, 1620, with about 100 passengers aboard. As the boat lay at anchor in Cape Cod Harbor, November 11, 1620, The Mayflower Compact was signed by forty-one men who were passengers on the *Mayflower*. A small group led by William Bradford were assigned to select a place for a permanent settlement. They landed December 21, 1620 at what is now Plymouth, Massachusetts.

Governor Bradford decreed that a three-day feast should be held. The first official Thanksgiving Day was set by Governor Bradford for Thursday, November 29, 1623.

The Pilgrims had something for which to be thankful. Divine Providence had guided them to a new world and had provided for them a new life. In spite of their severe losses, their great grief, and their innumerable hardships, the Pilgrims set aside a time for thanksgiving because they had something for which to give thanks.

This psalmist, possessed by a grateful heart, had something for which to give thanks, and he sang in verse 2: "Praise him for his mighty acts: praise him according to his excellent greatness." Regardless of how difficult our way may be, there is always something for which to give thanks.

Finally, a grateful heart finds:

Some Way in Which to Give Thanks

This psalmist was so grateful to God for the divine blessings that were upon him that he found many ways in which to show his thanksgiving. In verse 3 he said that he would praise God with the trumpet, psaltery, and harp. In verse 4 he said he would praise God with the timbrel, with dancing, with stringed instruments, and with organs. In verse 5 he said he would praise God with the loud cymbals.

He was simply showing us that when the heart is grateful it will find some way in which to give thanks to God for His blessings.

There are many ways in which we can do this. We do it by trusting in Christ as our Savior and by living obediently before Him. We do it by serving Him faithfully in various ways. We do it by our diligent daily study of his Word and by daily communion with Him in prayer. We do it by bringing our tithes and offerings and laying them upon His altar week by week. We do it by sharing Christ's love with others. There are many ways in which the grateful heart can give thanks to God for His many blessings. The grateful heart will find a way.

Conclusion

Dr. A. J. Cronin was a British doctor who gave up the practice of medicine to write novels. One time he told about a physician of his acquaintance who prescribed a "Thank-you cure" for frustrated and emotionally disturbed patients. When a defeated patient came to the doctor, Cronin said, and the doctor could find no physical symptoms, he would prescribe for the patient to say thank you for six weeks when anyone did him or her a favor. And, according to Cronin, the physician had a good cure rate. Finding a way to express thanksgiving helped to put them on the road to recovery.

The words *thanks* or *thanksgiving* appear about 140 times in the Bible. The Lord is telling us that He wants us to have a grateful heart and to find ways in which to express our gratitude to Him.

American author Fulton Oursler, once editor of *Reader's Digest,* died in 1952. Oursler told about a black nurse named Anna who took care of him when he was a little boy. A former slave, Anna had been freed and the Oursler family loved her as one of their own.

Oursler said that as a young boy he remembered seeing Anna, sitting at the kitchen table with her hands folded on her starched, white apron, looking up to heaven and praying, "Much obliged, Lord, for my vittles." When he asked Anna what vittles were, she said that vittles were what we had to eat and drink. Young Fulton told Anna that she would get her food whether or not she was thankful, and old Anna replied, "Sure, we'll get our vittles, but it makes 'm taste better when we's thankful."

Oursler said Anna told him that an old black preacher had taught her to be thankful as a little girl. He had told her to look for things for which to be thankful. Anna added that when she woke up in the morning, she would lie there "wondering what I've got to be thankful for. Then the smell of freshly perked coffee floats up the stairs and I knows I has something for which to be thankful. So, I begins my day with, 'Much obliged, Lord, for the coffee . . . and much obliged, too, for the smell of it.' "

The years passed and Oursler grew up and left home. One day he received a message that Anna was very sick and couldn't live much longer. Wanting to see his old nurse one more time, he traveled back to the old homeplace and when he walked into her bedroom he noticed her hands were folded over the white sheets as he had seen them folded on her white apron so many times before when she was praying. Oursler said that across the years he had become skeptical of God and spiritual things and he wondered as he looked at Anna what she had to be thankful for at a time like that. Then, as old Anna opened her eyes and looked around the room and saw so many of her longtime friends, she closed her eyes and said with a smile, "Much obliged, Lord, for such fine friends."

You see, there is always something for which to give thanks.

Note
1. J. Ralph Grant, *Word of the Lord for Special Days* (Grand Rapids: Baker Book House, 1964), p. 148.

Christian Baptism

Scripture: Acts 2:41

Introduction

In an issue of *Guideposts* magazine, well-known radio and TV commentator Paul Harvey told about his baptism.

In March 1972 Harvey and his wife were vacationing near Cave Creek, Arizona. One bright Sunday morning they drove to a little church on top of the hill and joined about a dozen others in worship. When the minister got up to preach he told the people he was going to talk about baptism, and Harvey said he yawned inside, expecting a boring sermon.

But as the minister spoke the Lord got hold of Harvey's heart. And when the invitation to respond was given, Harvey found himself walking down the aisle.

Although he had been saved as a youth, Harvey said he had never made a public profession of his faith. And though he knew there was no saving magic to the water, he said that when he was baptised he felt "immensely happy."

The joy Harvey felt in Christian baptism was also experienced by the converts on the day of Pentecost. Verse 41 declares it: "Then they that gladly received his word were baptized."

In this passage that sheds light on the doctrine of Christian baptism, let me point out to you some truths we need to examine.

What Precedes Baptism?

As summer precedes winter; as sowing precedes harvest; as nighttime precedes daylight, so there are some spiritual steps that precede baptism.

One must hear the Word of God.—"And with many other words did he testify and exhort, saying, Save yourselves from this unto-

105

ward generation" (Acts 2:40). As Peter preached, conviction came upon his hearers.

There can be no salvation without hearing the Word of God for "Faith cometh by hearing, and hearing by the word of God" (Rom. 10:17). Exposure to the Holy Scriptures always precedes conversation. Monica, Augustine's mother, was a devout Christian who prayed faithfully for her son's conversion. But Augustine was worldly, wicked, and would not have his mother's Savior. When Augustine moved from Carthage in North Africa to Milan, his mother dispaired, thinking he would never come to Christ. But the God who works in mysterious ways brought young Augustine under the influence of Ponticianus who was high in the emperor's court. Augustine's heart was deeply stirred as Ponticianus spoke about his conversion.

Going into the garden, Augustine seemed to hear a voice, saying, "Take up and read. Take up and read." Opening a Bible, his eyes fell on Romans 13:13-14: "Let us walk honestly, as in the day; not in rioting and drunkenness, not in chambering and wantonness, not in strife and envying, But put ye on the Lord Jesus Christ, and make not provision for the flesh, to fulfill the lusts thereof."

Augustine later wrote about what then happened: "No further would I read, nor needed I; for instantly at the end of this sentence, by a light, as it were, of serenity infused into my heart, all the darkness of doubt vanished away."[1]

Monica had followed her dissolute son to Milan. When he told her about his conversion, she knew her prayers had been answered. The following Easter he was baptized by Ambrose, the bishop of Milan. Hearing the Word of God led to Augustine's conversion.

One must personally accept Jesus Christ.—"Then they that gladly received his word were baptized" (Acts 2:41). As Luke showed, only those who had "gladly received his word" were baptized (John 5:24; Acts 9:1-22; 8:26-40). This is always the New Testament pattern. Baptism follows repentance from sin and faith in Jesus Christ. To repent is to turn from sin (Mark 1:15); to believe is to accept Christ by faith (Eph. 2:8-10).

One of the truly great early Baptists of the United States was John A. Broadus. Born in Culpeper County, Virginia, in 1827,

Broadus served The Southern Baptist Theological Seminary, Louisville, Kentucky, both as a professor and as its president.

He was saved when he was about sixteen in a revival meeting at Virginia's Mt. Poney Baptist Church. The next day he heard S. M. Poindexter preach on the parable of the talents and came to the conclusion that God was calling him to preach. Shortly after his conversion, Broadus was baptized in Mountain Run Stream into the fellowship of the Mt. Poney Baptist Church.

The New Testament pattern is always repentance, faith, and regeneration, then baptism. This order is never reversed (Acts 16:14-15,30-34).

What Is the Purpose of Baptism?

In his book *Christian Doctrine*, the late W. T. Connor wrote: "We maintain that the fundamental facts of the gospel are the Death and Resurrection of Jesus as the ground of our salvation and that baptism is meant to set forth these facts."[2]

Baptism symbolizes three truths:

It symbolizes the burial and resurrection of Christ.—"Know ye not, that so many of us as were baptized into Jesus Christ were baptized into his death? Therefore we are buried with him by baptism into death: that like as Christ was raised up from the dead by the glory of the Father, even so we also should walk in newness of life" (Rom. 6:3-4; see also v. 11). The visitor to Paris can see Napoleon's huge, red granite tomb in the Hotel des Invalides. It is thirteen feet long, six and one-half feet wide, and fourteen and one-half feet high. In it are the remains of the "Little Corporal" who was brought to his knees by the Duke of Wellington at Waterloo in 1815. Once master of all Europe, "He was cursed as a despot, blessed as the embodiment of progress and order," as Lowell Thomas put it. However, the great Napoleon who rewrote history by conquering Europe has not conquered the grave. But Jesus Christ, the humblest of men, was nailed to His cross on Friday and raised from the dead on Easter morning. Christ has conquered the grave and Christian baptism is a testimony to that.

It symbolizes the believer's death to sin and resurrection to a new life in Christ.—"Know ye not, that so many of us as were baptized into Jesus Christ were baptized into his death (Rom.

6:3)?" "Knowing this, that our old man is crucified with him, that the body of sin might be destroyed, that henceforth we should not serve sin. Now if we be dead with Christ, we believe that we shall also live with him" (vv. 6,8). Augustine, the fourth-century church father, was a sinful profligate until he was saved. One day after his conversion—so the story relates—Augustine met one of his former mistresses on the street. When he recognized her, Augustine turned around and hurried off in the opposite direction, but she called out, "Augustine, it is I." And Augustine called back, "Yes, I know, but it is not I." He meant that he had died to the old way of life and had been raised to a new life in Christ. Baptism symbolizes this.

It symbolizes our resurrection when Jesus comes.—"Now if we be dead with Christ, we believe that we shall also live with Him: Knowing that Christ being raised from the dead dieth no more; death hath no more dominion over him" (Rom. 6:8-9). When London's great preacher, F. B. Meyer, died, his funeral service was one of joy. Hymns and Scriptures on the resurrection were sung and read. At the end of the service, no funeral march was played. Instead, the organist played the thunderous chords of the Halleujah Chorus. Because of the promise of our resurrection, the Christian can face death triumphantly.

What Is the Proper Mode for Baptism?

General Sam Houston was the first president of Texas. He also served as a United States senator from that state. After he made his profession of faith in Jesus Christ, influenced in his decision by his godly wife, Houston returned to Texas where he presented himself for baptism. On November 19, 1854, he was baptized by Dr. Rufus C. Burleson into the fellowship of the Independence Baptist Church. According to D. D. Tidwell, writing in *The Quarterly Review* for October, November, and December, 1967: "It is said that he [Houston] deliberately kept his purse on his person when immersed in order that his pocketbook might also be baptized."[3]

Several modes of baptism have been practiced through the years. Among them are immersion, sprinkling, pouring, and dipping. But what is the proper mode for baptism according to the New Testament?

The English word *baptize* is not an English word at all. It is a Greek word that has been Anglicized. The Greek word is *baptizo*.

According to Thayer's Greek-English Lexicon, *baptizo* means, "to dip repeatedly, to immerge, submerge . . . an immersion in water."

On the other hand, the word *sprinkle* is *rantizo*. Used in Hebrews 9:13,19,21-22, it refers to being sprinkled with blood, not water. "Sprinkling" which is used in Hebrews 11:28; 12:24; and 1 Peter 1:2 also is a sprinkling with blood, not water. Therefore it must be said in all honesty that sprinkling in the New Testament never refers to water baptism.

In the *Encyclopedia of Southern Baptists,* T. C. Smith, writing on the subject of baptism, declares: "That immersion was the correct form of baptism in New Testament times is supported by the Greek word *baptizo,* which means 'to dip' or 'to plunge.' For the apostle Paul nothing but immersion could express an identification with Christ in his death, burial, and resurrection (Rom. 6:3 ff.). . . . It is admitted that, at the beginning of the second century A.D., pouring was allowed if circumstances arose where immersion was found to be impossible, but the author of Didache, our source for this information, nowhere suggested that this mode could prevail as normative for Christians.

"Reliable New Testament scholars of both Protestant and Catholic communions readily admit that the New Testament evidence unquestionably sets forth immersion as the proper mode for Christian baptism. When they employ the modes of sprinkling or pouring, they do so, not on the basis of New Testament authority, but for the sake of convenience or in consideration of the health of the individual to be baptized."[4]

This mode of baptism was what was in Luke's mind when he wrote in Acts 2:41: "Then they that gladly received his word were baptized."

What Should Follow Baptism?

"And the same day there were added unto them three thousand souls" (Acts 2:41b-47).

Several things should follow Christian baptism:

Church membership.—"And the same day there were added unto them about three thousand souls" (v. 47). "Them" refers to the believers who made up the Jerusalem church (see Acts 1—2). Although there are instances in Acts where, apparently, some converts were baptized without becoming members of a local church, the fully developed New Testament plan shows that baptism, upon repentance from sin and faith in Christ, admits one to church membership. Henry Clarence Thiessen, in *An Introduction to the New Testament,* writes: "The disciples were to begin witnessing in Jerusalem, to go on to Judaea and Samaria, and finally to the ends of the earth (Acts 1:8). The Book of Acts shows how they carried out this command."[5] Then Thiessen adds: "Shortly thereafter this church had increased to where it had 5,000 men (Greek, *andrōn*) alone (4:4); a little later we read that multitudes, both of men and women, were added to the Lord (5:14), and once again that the number of the disciples was multiplying (6:1). Lawson asks: 'Would it be too much to say that there were twenty thousand Jews in Jerusalem who believed that Jesus Christ was the promised Messiah, King, Priest, and Prophet?' "[6] The church at Jerusalem continued to grow as people were added to it by baptism.

Growth in grace.—"And they continued steadfastly in the apostles' doctrine" (v. 42). Discipleship was a vital part of the Jerusalem church's ministry. Those who were baptized continued to grow in grace and discipleship as they were taught by the apostles.

According to *Time* magazine, going to church is good for one's health. The magazine reported that people who go to church regularly have less arteriosclerotic heart disease and bronchitis. It also reported that perhaps hymn singing helps to "clear the tubes." Also, regular church attendance reduces incidences of cirrhosis of the liver, tuberculosis, cancer of the cervix, suicides, and one-car fatal accidents. But a spiritual plus from regular church attendance is growing in Christ's likeness. Growth in grace —Christlikeness—should follow baptism.

Fellowship.—"And all that believed were together, and had all things common; And sold their possessions and goods and parted them to all men, as every man had need" (vv. 44-45). Halford E.

Luccock wrote: "The leader of a mountain-climbing group which ascended Mt. Everest writes, 'Morale was evidently high. Most satisfactory of all was to observe how our friendship and confidence in each other had increased. We had been together on the rope, and had had reason to respect each other's prowess.' In the fellowship of Christ, men and women had 'been together on the rope.' Their spirits were tied together.' "[7]

Joy.—"Did eat their meat with gladness and singleness of heart" (v. 46). Tertullian, born in Carthage, North Africa, about AD 160, wrote about the early church: "Its members rejoiced, and its persecutors complained, that its teachings spread like wildfire. 'We are but of yesterday,' wrote Tertullian, 'yet we have filled your cities, islands, towns, and burrows; we are in the camp, the senate and the forum. Our foes lament that every sex, age and condition, and persons of every rank, are converts to the name of Christ.' " These early Christians were characterized by joy, and the church grew as a result. Some speaker to whom I was listening said that about seventy times the New Testament enjoins Christians to be joyful.

Joseph Haydn (1732-1809), the noted Austrian composer, was once asked why his church music was so cheerful. And Haydn replied, "I cannot make it otherwise. I write as I feel. When I think upon God, my heart is so full of joy that the notes dance and leap, as it were, from my pen."[8]

According to *Parade* magazine, William Linkhaw, a North Carolina man, was convicted in 1873 of disrupting church services with his singing. His Methodist brethren said they had put up with him for years and that even when everyone else had stopped singing Linkhaw kept on. When Linkhaw was asked to be quiet, he refused saying that singing was part of his duty to God. But the courts found him guilty of a misdemeanor and ordered him to keep quiet. However, when he appealed the conviction to the state supreme court it was overturned. Linkhaw may not have been much of a singer, but he had the right idea: being a Christian ought to be a joyous experience.

Conclusion

Ann and Adoniram Judson were the first Baptist foreign missionaries from the United States. He was a Congregationalist minister reared in Massachusetts, who sailed with his wife for Indian in February 1812. But as he sailed toward India (and a meeting with Baptist missionary William Carey), Judson studied his New Testament and came to the conviction that only those who were responsible should be baptized and that it should be by immersion. So, when he and his wife landed at Calcutta, they were both baptized by immersion and sent word back to the American Congregational Board in Massachusetts that they were now Baptists.

Notes
1. Walter Russell Bowie, *Man of Fire, Torchbearers of the Gospel* (New York: Harper and Row, 1961), p. 81.
2. W. T. Conner, *Christian Doctrine* (Nashville: Broadman Press, 1937), p. 281.
3. *The Quarterly Review*, Oct., Nov., Dec., 1967, p. 241.
4. *Encyclopedia of Southern Baptists*, Vol. 1 (Nashville: Broadman Press, 1958), p. 108.
5. Henry Clarence Thiessen, *An Introduction to the New Testament* (Grand Rapids: Wm. B. Eerdmans Publishing Co., 1951), p. 36.
6. Ibid., p. 36.
7. Halford E. Luccock, *More Preaching Values in the Epistles of Paul, Vol. II, II Corinthians, Galatians, Philippians, Colossians* (New York: Harper and Row Publishers, 1961), p. 216.
8. F. B. Meyers, *Psalms, Bible Readings* (Grand Rapids: Zondervan Publishing House, n.d.), p. 45.

Life's Fountain of Youth*

Scripture: Psalm 103:5

Introduction

I imagine Ponce de Leon drank more water than anyone in history! He came to America with Columbus on the explorer's second voyage in 1493. In 1508, he returned to the New World and conquered Puerto Rico. In 1510, he became its governor.

Indians in the New World told de Leon about an island named Bimini where there was a magical fountain. Anyone who drank from that fountain, the Indians said, would have his youth restored.

For years the Spaniard dreamed about finding this wonderful fountain. Finally, in 1513, he fitted out an expedition to look for fabled Bimini. On March 27, 1513, he sighted land. On April 2 he landed and called his new discovery "Florida."

Although he drank from every spring he came across while exploring Florida, he never discovered the magical fountain of youth. His search was long and disappointing.

Mankind has been looking for the fountain of youth ever since. Everybody wants to stay young. The quest for youth is universal and timeless. Novelists have written about it. Balladeers have sung about it. Poets have dreamed about it. Everybody wants to stay young.

Cosmeticians have built multimillion dollar businesses telling people how to do it. Exercise enthusiasts have sold millions of dollars worth of books and equipment, showing people how to do it. Health food manufacturers have built huge businesses producing special foods that promise it. I think there is nothing in the human heart that troubles us more, or claims more of our energies and attentions, than this business of trying to stay young.

113

Some of our greatest writers have written about this dream. Oliver Wendell Holmes pictured the old man saying:

> Oh for one hour of youthful joy!
>   Give back my twentieth spring!
> I'd rather laugh, a bright-haired boy
>   Than reign, a gray-beard king.

I think, however, that we must put things in perspective. Age is not just the accumulation of years and youth is not just a lack of years. More is involved. In a true sense, both age and youth are attitudes of mind. Some people are old at twenty; others are young at eighty.

Writing about this, Holmes stated: "To be seventy years young is sometimes far more cheerful and hopeful than to be forty years old."

The Bible has something to say about staying young. It points us to life's fountain of youth and encourages us to drink deeply.

Although Robert Browning's philosophy was "Grow old along with me! The best is yet to be," the psalmist's philosophy was: "[God] satisfieth thy mouth with good things; so that thy youth is renewed like the eagle's" (Ps. 103:5).

This psalmist had often seen eagles soaring high on the air currents. They never seemed to grow weary or to lose their strength. They seemed never to grow old. Watching them, the psalmist might have said to himself: "God supplies strength and youth to the eagles. He will do the same thing for me. I will ask him to keep me young as he keeps the eagles young."

This is the fountain of youth from which the Heavenly Father invites us to drink. Although not even God will turn back the hands of time and remove the wrinkles from our face, He can and will put a song in our heart and keep us young in spirit. He will lead us to life's fountain of youth and restore us if we will trust Him.

If we would drink from life's fountain of youth:

We Must Keep Our Life Clean

Recently, I read an article in a Nashville, Tennessee, newspaper, titled, "High Cost of Small Crimes." The article stated that a criminal court in Bangkok, Thailand, had sentenced a man to five years in prison and another man to eighteen months for illegal possession of heroin—one fiftieth of a gram! On Bangkok's open market, it was worth only about three cents.

All sins are costly—the "little" ones as well as the "big" ones. Each has built into it a hardening, deadly touch.

In his "Epistle to a Young Friend," Robert Burns pointed this out when he wrote:

> But, och! It hardens a' within,
> And petrifies the feeling!

Nothing wrinkles, ruins, and destroys as does sin. The Satan of the Bible is very old and cynical, and everyone who serves him becomes like him. Sin hardens all it touches and exacts a heavy price.

English poet Lord Byron—worldly, lustful—sighed beneath the weight of his thirty-six years:

> My days are in the yellow leaf;
>   The flowers and fruits of love are gone;
> The worm, the canker, and the grief
>   are mine alone!

Sin ages its devotees! To drink from life's fountain of youth, we must keep our life clean. Our prayer must be that of King David: "Create in me a clean heart, O God; and renew a right spirit within me" (Ps. 51:10).

Secondly, if we would drink from life's fountain of youth:

We Must Keep Our Enthusiasm

Henry Alford Porter, in his book, *Toward the Sunrising,* said that poet James Russell Lowell was always "bubbling over with enthusiasm."

Living during America's darkest days, Lowell saw his beloved land divided by the terrible Civil War. On every hand there was agony and heartache. But in spite of the darkness, Lowell never lost his zest for life. It was inextinguishable!

One day Lowell and a friend were walking on the outskirts of Boston when they passed an institution bearing the name, "Home for Incurable Children." With a twinkle in his eye, Lowell said to his friend: "Ah, . . . they'll get me in there yet. That is just what he was"—an incurable child at heart.

If we are to stay young at heart, we must keep our enthusiasm for life. If we do, we shall live in the sweet-smelling forest of perpetual youth and life's fountain of youth shall continuously restore us.

What does it matter if our bones are arthritic, our eyesight is dim, our walk is slow, and our digestion is poor? There are a lot of eighteen-year-olds who don't have good health. But if we keep our enthusiasm for life, we shall still be young at ninety!

Nothing is more necessary for a happy, well-balanced life than enthusiasm. One day a man was planting an apple tree in his backyard. He was not young in years, for he had already passed his seventieth birthday. Next door there lived a man who was about the same age, but their outlook on life was poles apart. The man planting the apple tree was always enthusiastic. But his neighbor constantly camped on yesterday's doorstep. The first man's spirit was sweet and gentle. The second man's spirit was bitter and senile.

The sour neighbor watched as his friend planted the tender, green apple tree.

"Why are you planting that thing? As old as you are you will never live to eat apples from it," he sneered.

His friend looked up, smiled, and said: "You may be right. I may never eat apples from this tree. But tomorrow is coming and someone who likes apples is going to eat apples from the tree I planted."

Paul Laurence Dunbar, a gifted American Negro poet, writes about the person who has lost his enthusiasm for life. He has this poor, brother lamenting:

> A crust of bread and a corner to sleep in,
> A minute to smile and an hour to weep in,
> A pint of joy to a peck of trouble,
> And never a laugh but the moans come double:
> And that is life.[1]

No friends, that's not life! That's senility, bitterness, and old age. Here is life:

> A crust and corner that love makes precious
> With the smile to warm and the tears to refresh us;
> And joy seems sweeter when cares come after,
> And a moan is the finest foil for laughter;
> And that is life.[2]

Look at your skin. It's wrinkled, isn't it. Look at your hands. They have age spots on them, don't they? Take off your glasses and look around you. The people all disappear don't they? But those things don't mean you're getting old. They just mean you have been here a good while.

Drink at life's fountain of youth. Keep your enthusiasm and you will never grow old!

If we would drink from life's fountain of youth:

We Must Live with a Purpose

One day the president of California's Stanford University was driving down a long, hot, California highway when he came upon a tramp. Stopping the car, the educator called out, "Say, friend, how about a ride?"

"No, thank you," the sweltering traveler slowly replied. "Since I ain't going nowhere I ain't in no hurry to get there."

A lot of folks have that problem. They have no purpose in life. They don't live. They just exist.

I am amazed at the long list of people, well up in years, who accomplished so much because they lived with a purpose. Kant was still writing when he was past seventy. Victor Hugo astounded the world with some of his best literary gems when he was eighty. Tennyson wrote "Crossing the Bar" when he was eighty. Benjamin Franklin rendered great service to his country after he passed his sixtieth birthday. Winston Churchill, the savior of Europe, would have been a failure if he had died before he was sixty-five.

Also, Palmerston, at eighty-one, was Prime Minister of England. Bismarck was leading Germany when he was seventy-four. Christy was premier of Italy when he was seventy-five. Verdi was writing operas when he was past eighty. Titian painted his incomparable picture, *The Battle of Lepanto,* when he was ninety-eight. He painted his *Last Supper* when he was ninety-nine. Michelangelo was still producing masterpieces when he was eighty-nine. Monet was painting award-winning masterpieces when he was eighty-five. Thomas A. Edison was busily seeking out new inventions when he died at eighty-five. Commandore Vanderbilt acquired most of his railroads when he was well past seventy. At ninety, Sophocles wrote *Oedipus.* Oliver Wendell Holmes, Bernard Baruch, Henry Ford, Toscanini, and Herbert Hoover reached new heights of accomplishment after they were eighty.

Do not these striking encouragements from history clearly show us that one who lives with a great purpose locked up in his heart will never grow old? One cannot live a healthy life when one has no purpose for living. Listen to Victor Hugo. It is the shout of the victor: "Winter is on my head, but eternal spring is in my heart."

Finally, to drink from the fountain of youth:

We Must Keep in Touch with God

Dr. Walter Brooks was a Negro Baptist preacher. He was pastor of the Nineteenth Street Baptist Church of Washington, D.C., for more than sixty years. He was born a slave, in the city of Richmond, Virginia. When he was fourteen, he received his freedom and shortly thereafter began to preach as a Presbyterian minister. But he fell in love with a young woman who was a Baptist, and, as happens so often, she won his heart and changed his mind. Soon he joined a Baptist church and became a Baptist minister.

After he had served the Washington church for thirty years, he decided to resign. Getting down on his knees to pray, Brooks told the Lord he was going to resign because he thought the church needed a younger man.

But, Brooks later said, the Lord asked why He couldn't make me a young man.

Then, drinking from the divine fountain of youth, Brooks stayed another thirty years—past his ninetieth birthday!

Like the psalmist who stayed in touch with God, Brooks' strength was renewed like the eagle's. He kept young because he kept in touch with God.

Conclusion

When I was a boy in Sunday School, my teacher always referred to the Heavenly Father as "the Old Man upstairs." So I grew up thinking of God as very old, with white hair, and a long, white beard.

But that's a false conception of God.

The God of the Bible is the very image of power, strength, and youthfulness. When He chose to reveal himself, He did not come as an old, worn-out man. He incarnated Himself in the flesh of a baby. He ministered to people in the flesh of a young man whose name is Jesus Christ.

This Savior whom the Book of Hebrews calls the exact image of God, walked across Palestine with the vigorous, long, powerful stride of a young man. He walked on the stormy sea. With strong hands He broke the bread of the boy and served it to the hungry multitude. He drove the money changers out of the Temple. He attended the wedding of a young couple in Cana. He often prayed all night. He was a strong, young man who kept in constant touch with the Eternal Fountain of Youth.

Isaiah gave us the precious secret that Jesus knew. Isaiah told us to keep in touch with God and we would never grow old: "But they that wait upon the Lord shall renew their strength; they shall mount up with wings as eagles; they shall run, and not be weary; and they shall walk, and not faint" (Isa. 40:31).

To grow old is inexcusable! Keep in touch with the ageless God. Drink from His fountain of youth, for He promises: "[He will satisfy] thy mouth with good things; so that thy youth is renewed like the eagle's" (Ps. 103:5).

Notes

*I acknowledge my debt to Henry Alford Porter who gave me the inspiration for this sermon: *Toward the Sunrising* (Nashville: Broadman Press, 1947), pp. 114-122.

1. *The Complete Poems of Paul Laurence Dunbar* (New York: Dodd, Mead & Co., 1913).

2. Ibid.

The Meaning of Christmas

Scripture: Luke 2:1-20

Introduction

Before Oliver Cromwell and the Puritans came to power in England in 1642, Christmas was England's happiest holiday.

But when Cromwell came to power, the Puritan ministers preached against Christmas merriment, blasting it as a heathen practice. They said Jesus wouldn't approve of the celebration.

During the Middle Ages in England, Christmas was observed by everyone from the beggar in his hovel to the king in his palace. And many notable events took place at the Christmas season.

King Henry II was crowned on Christmas Day, AD 1154. King John signed the Magna Charta on Christmas Day, AD 1214. And at the Christmas season in AD 1348, Edward III established the still-famous "Order of the Garter."

Also, King Richard II gave a lavish party for his friend, the King of Armenia, at Christmas. Both the first British comedy and the earliest British tragedy were performed on the stage on Christmas Day, AD 1561. And the English stage got its start at Christmas time when Queen Elizabeth, the daughter of King Henry VIII, organized actors and presented Christmas plays at Greenwich and Hampton Court.

But the Reformation was having its effect by the time the Stuarts came to power. The hard-line Calvinists refused to let the people enjoy Christmas festivities, saying that observing Christ's birthday was not scriptural. And, under Oliver Cromwell, Parliament passed a state law prohibiting religious festivals and the celebrating of Christ's nativity.

It was not uncommon in England during that era for town criers to go through their communities calling out loudly so that every possible offender could hear, "No Christmas! No Christmas!"

120

I have no trouble with festivities at the Christmas season, for it is a happy time. But the crowning of a king or the writing of the Magna Charta or the establishing of the "Order of the Garter" at Christmas is not the most important thing that ever happened at that holy season.

This text from Luke's Gospel pinpoints for us the meaning of Christmas: it is the birthday of our Lord Jesus Christ. Let me, therefore, suggest to you that Christmas finds its true meaning in the humble manger, the holy name, and the heavenly miracle.

The Humble Manger

Great people are often born in humble circumstances. Great hearts often beat beneath the rags of poverty. Humble birthplaces have cradled the majority of the world's great leaders.

Shakespeare, that bright luminaire of literature, was born in a humble home at Stratford-on-Avon. Columbus, who discovered the new world, was born in poverty at Genoa. Lincoln, the Great Emancipator, was born in a roughly hewn log cabin and was then covered with a bearskin.

And from an obscure corner of the globe, in a stall where animals were kept for weary travelers, the golden hinge on which the ages turn was born. "And she brought forth her firstborn son, and wrapped him in swaddling clothes, and laid him in a manger."

It was divinely provided.—"And laid him in a manger" (v. 7*b*).

It was divinely protected.—"Because there was no room for them in the inn" (v. 7*c*). Nazareth's inn was full, but the empty manger was protected for the Son by the Father.

The Holy Name

In the holy Scriptures, the Lord Jesus is called by perhaps as many as 300 names. In this text He is called "her firstborn son" (v. 7); "a Saviour" (v. 11); "babe" (vv. 12,16); and "child" (v. 17).

Names mean something. The Scriptures use two very significant names for Jesus: Emmanuel and Jesus.

Emmanuel.—Three times in the Scriptures this name appears: Isaiah 7:14; 8:8; and Matthew 1:23. It means "God with us."

In the humble manger that night, God came down to us—bone of our bone and flesh of our flesh—one with us. But in coming to the earth, God did not lose His diety. Rather, He took on our humanity. In Jesus Christ we have God in the flesh with us!

Jesus means "Yahweh is salvation"—He is both God and Savior. "Jesus" appears in every New Testament book except Jude. The Old Testament declares Him; the New Testament reveals Him.

The late R. C. Campbell told about Joseph Palworth, one of the characters in a novel written by George McDonald.

Palworth had decided to read through the New Testament. He said he had no definite ideal in the resolve when he started on his project; it just seemed like "a good thing to do." He said he felt it would help him keep in touch "with things above."

Palworth began with the table of genealogies in the first chapter of Matthew. "But when I came to the twenty-first verse and read, 'Thou shalt call his name Jesus: for he shall save his people from their sins,' I fell on my knees. . . . Here was news of One who came from behind the root of sin to deliver me from that in me which made being a bad thing! . . . Suffice it that from that moment I was a student, a disciple."[1]

The Heavenly Miracle

The day of miracles has not passed although some theologians say it has. Miracles happen around us every day and often we are blind to them.

The miracle of His birth.—This is the greatest of all miracles. Isaiah had prophesied the virgin birth of a Savior: "Therefore the Lord himself shall give you a sign; Behold, a virgin shall conceive and bear a son, and shall call his name Immanuel" (Isa. 7:14). Matthew recorded the virgin birth in Matthew 1:18: "Now the birth of Jesus Christ was on this wise: When his mother Mary was espoused to Joseph, before they came together, she was found with child of the Holy Ghost."

How can we understand this greatest mystery of a book that is full of mysteries? We can't! We accept it by faith. Henry Drummond, the great English lay preacher, once said: "There are so many more mysteries outside of the Bible than there are in it, that I have ceased to worry over those in it."

The miracle of timing.—His birth is pinpointed in history: Caesar Augustus was on the Roman throne (Luke 2:1); it came during the first reign of Cyrenius, the governor of Syria (v. 2); it came during a known period of national taxation (v. 3); and it came where it was divinely prophesied (Mic. 5:2). Although Mary and Joseph lived at Nazareth, the taxation of Caesar Augustus moved them to Bethlehem and their divine rendezvous with prophecy.

The miracle of the heavenly host.—During World War II, when American Captain Eddie Rickenbacker had to ditch his plane in the Pacific, he and his men drifted helplessly for twenty-one days. Lieutenant Whittaker, the copilot, wrote a book about their days adrift titled, *We Thought We Heard the Angels Sing.*

But the shepherds actually heard the angels sing on Judea's silent hillsides the night Jesus was born: "Glory to God in the highest, and on earth peace, good will toward men." And while the melody of the heavenly host was still trembling on the night air, the humble shepherds went to Bethlehem and found the promised Messiah in the manger.

Conclusion

Christmas finds its meaning in the birth of Jesus Christ. "He wrote no books; composed no poems; gave birth to no elaborate code of laws; led no army; established no wordly empire; invented no scientific appliance; spent but three brief years in public life; was put to death as a malefactor amid the insults and yells of an infuriated mob. Yet he has wielded, and still wields in the world, a power and influence unequalled by the combined influence and power of all the famous monarchs, statesmen, generals, inventors, and authors the world has seen. The name of Jesus sounds down the corridors of the centuries like the music of all choirs visible and invisible, poured forth in one anthem. His name blossoms on the pages of history like the flowers of one thousand springtimes blossoming the narrow limits of one garden. His influence, like spice-gales from heaven, perfumes the air of all continents."[2]

This is what Christmas is all about.

Notes

1. R. C. Campbell, *The Christ of the Centuries* (Nashville: Broadman Press, 1947), p. 7.

2. Robert G. Lee, *The Sinner's Savior* (Nashville: Broadman Press, 1950), p. 89.

Index of Illustrations